Serve from the Heart

Finding Your Gifts and Talents for Service

LEADER'S KIT

CHURCH OF THE
RESURRECTION
RESOURCES

Abingdon Press

Foreword

I have an old toolbox that belonged to my great grandfather, Joseph Lorson. He was a carpenter who built homes in Kansas City in the early 1900's. Inside are a myriad of antique tools. Some of the tools I recognize. Others are more mysterious to me—I am not sure how they were used or what purpose they served.

As I look through his bin I am surprised by what seems to be a duplication of tools—there are a half a dozen saws—each slightly different in size or cutting blade. There are different kinds and shapes of chisels and planes. I would love to know when my great grandfather used this particular tool as opposed to that one.

I have debated about what to do with these tools. They were passed on to me by my father as a legacy—a gift. Should I mount them on a special wall—a tribute to my family heritage? Perhaps I should carefully preserve them in their box to pass on to my children? Uncertain about what to do with them, they sit in their wooden toolbox in one corner of my garage.

But every once in awhile I have a need for one of these tools—usually for a saw, but sometimes a chisel or a hammer—and carefully I take one of these tools from the bin, and put it to use. And instantly there is a sense of satisfaction as the tool does exactly what it was made to do—these tools were designed to be used! They were designed to work. These tools were meant to build things!

I have also come to appreciate the nuances between some of these tools. The small thin blade of the trim saw was perfect when I needed to replace a piece of molding in my study. But the large hand saw did the trick when branches were broken and hanging from my trees during an ice storm.

Of course the metaphors are apparent - each of us have been given gifts by the Holy Spirit—spiritual tools. Some of the gifts are mysterious—we are not exactly sure how they work or what purpose they serve. Others are readily identified and easy to use. But all are meant to be used, and not simply kept safely hidden away.

What is more, when we understand what spiritual gifts may be needed for a particular kind of task in the church, help persons identify their spiritual gifts, and then align the right people for the right tasks, the work of the ministry is more effective, and those doing the ministry receive great joy—for they have found the very thing they were gifted for. It is amazing the difference the right tool can make when approaching a difficult task.

Carol Cartmill and Yvonne Gentile have done a remarkable job of helping hundreds of people to discover their spiritual gifts and to begin using them within the church. As a result of their efforts our people are more effectively serving God, the ministry is growing and expanding, and our members are discovering joy, not drudgery, in their ministry for Christ.

This book is an excellent guide to discovering and making the most of the tools that the Holy Spirit places in our toolbins.

Adam Hamilton
Senior Pastor, The United Methodist
Church of the Resurrection

Contents

Teaching Serving from the Heart Using the Leader Book and CD-ROM

Welcome to *Serving from the Heart: Finding Your Gifts and Talents for Service.* You have a variety of tools to choose from as you prepare to lead your group. The **Leader Kit** includes this leader book and an enhanced CD-ROM inside the back cover sleeve.

This **Leader Book** includes both teaching plans for each of the sessions plus all eight chapters included in the participant's workbook.

There are eight session plans in the leader book. Each leader session plan includes the *objective* for the session, helps for *preparing* including video segments to view and other suggested ways to use the CD-ROM, *materials* you need to gather, a *welcome* and a *prayer*. Several group and individual activities are provided with step by step instructions and time needed to complete each.

Following each session plan, you have the entire text from the chapter(s) from the participant workbook that you cover in that session.

The **CD-ROM** includes helps to use in preparing, conducting and promoting your group study:

■ Nine clips for leaders: first hand advice straight from Carol Cartmill and Yvonne Gentile of the Church of the Resurrection, authors of the study.

■ Eight sets of overhead slides to use either printed onto transparencies or projected.

■ A digital photo slide show for use (either printed or projected) in Session 6 on Dreams

■ Four handouts to print or customize for class use including the forms for the slide show, Ministry Profile, Strengths Bombardment exercise and Ministry Matching exercise.

■ A promotional poster announcing your Serving from the Heart study printable on home or professional printers.

■ Four music tracks (2 vocal, 2 instrumental) for use during class activities or as closings.

Class Sessions

Serving from the Heart can be taught in eight 45-60 minute sessions or in four longer, 2 hour sessions – or combined for weekend retreats. The following outline may help you plan your sessions. The leader sessions are in bold and the accompanying participant chapters are in italics.

45 to 60 minute format	120 minute format
Session 1: Spiritual Gifts: Biblical Foundation *Participant Chapter 1*	**Session 1: Spiritual Gifts: Biblical Foundation** *Participant Chapter 1* **Session 2: Spiritual Gifts Discovery Tool** *(No Participant Chapter)*
Session 2: Spiritual Gifts Discovery Tool *(No Participant Chapter)*	**Session 3: Spiritual Gifts Defined** *Participant Chapter 2* **Session 4: Talents and Resources** *Participant Chapters 3 and 4*
Session 3: Spiritual Gifts Defined *Participant Chapter 2*	**Session 5: Individuality** *Participant Chapter 5* **Session 6: Dreams** *Participant Chapter 6*
Session 4: Talents and Resources *Participant Chapters 3 and 4*	**Session 7: Experiences** *Participant Chapter 7* **Session 8: Putting it All Together** *Participant Chapter 8*
Session 5: Individuality *Participant Chapter 5*	
Session 6: Dreams *Participant Chapter 6*	
Session 7: Experiences *Participant Chapter 7*	
Session 8: Putting it All Together *Participant Chapter 8*	

INTRODUCTION AND BIBLICAL FOUNDATION

OBJECTIVE FOR THIS SESSION:

To gain a biblical foundation for understanding spiritual gifts.

Prepare by reading in advance the material in the Introduction and Chapter 1 in the workbook, and in Session 1 in the leader's guide. Read all Bible passages for yourself. Try all instructions given both in the workbook and the leader's guide.

Watch the CD rom video segment, "Chapter 1, Spiritual Gifts." As you prepare for the class, you might also enjoy watching the video for Chapter 8 and the Conclusion for an overview of the class and its benefits. If you are using the overhead slides, either print the overheads for Session 1 for use on a projector or bring the disk to use with a computer and projector.

Materials Needed: blank nametags; pens or pencils; white board or newsprint with appropriate markers; Bibles; workbooks

As participants arrive, hand them their workbooks and ask them to make a nametag for themselves.

Welcome and Introduce (5 minutes)

Welcome everyone to *Serving from the Heart*. Explain that it is an eight-week continuing course (*four-week if you have chosen to combine sessions into two-hour segments). Let them know that at the end of the course, they will have learned about spiritual gifts, had an opportunity to work at identifying their own spiritual gifts, and begun to identify just what their own place of service and ministry within the church might be.

Introduce yourself first, and then have the class members introduce themselves. You might have each class member say how long they have been a member of your congregation and tell what has been their most recent experience serving in a ministry either within your own, a previous congregation, or in the community. Be prepared to hear both positive and negative experiences! One reason for this course is to enhance the likelihood that persons will have positive ministry experiences as they serve in the places that better utilize their God-given spiritual gifts.

Pray (2 minutes)

Offer this prayer or one like it:

Gracious God: We ask that you be with us during this adventure of exploring our spiritual gifts. May we focus on ways that we might better serve you and your people. Help us remember that our gifts have been given for your glory and for the building of your Kingdom. In Christ's name we pray. Amen.

Introduce the S.T.R.I.D.E. Concept (8 minutes)

Ask participants quickly to brainstorm reasons they have heard (or used themselves) for why people do not volunteer to serve in the church. List these on the white board or newsprint. Share that most of these reasons melt away when a person's spiritual gifts are used and their passions are engaged in ministries.

The goal of this course is not the recruitment of volunteers. Instead it is to help people discover their God-given S.T.R.I.D.E., and to help them find ways to use their spiritual gifts in effective and fulfilling places of service. S.T.R.I.D.E is an acronym used to capture the gifts, skills and resources we will explore together in this study. Not only has God called us all to serve, but God has also designed us in such a way that we could serve in an area where we would be not only capable but also happy to serve!

Summarizing the material from the workbook, explain the S.T.R.I.D.E. concept:

    S – Spiritual gifts
    T – Talents
    R – Resources
    I – Individuality
    D – Dreams
    E – Experiences

All of these are part of who we are, and can be used for God's purposes. We'll start in this course with spiritual gifts.

You as the leader may be tempted to define the term *spiritual gifts* for the participants here, but it may be more helpful to refrain from doing so. Instead, allow the participants to summarize a description of *spiritual gifts* at the end of the session from what they find in their Bible study.

Study the Bible *(25 minutes)*

Divide your group into an even number of smaller groups, each with three to five members. Ask everyone to turn to page 7 in the workbook where the questions on the four foundational Bible passages dealing with spiritual gifts are found. Ask half of the groups to work on the questions dealing with 1 Corinthians 12 and Romans 12:1-8. Ask the other half of the groups to work on the questions dealing with Ephesians 4:1-16 and 1 Peter 4:10-11. If you have 4 or more groups, you may want to have each group work with a different passage. After making

sure everyone has a Bible, allow fifteen minutes for groups to work on these questions.

Stop after fifteen minutes, even if the groups are not quite done. Then work through the questions, allowing the group members to provide the answers as much as possible.

An answer key is provided here, based on the New Revised Standard Version of the Bible:

---

1 Corinthians 12

According to verse 1, what is Paul's desire regarding the subject of spiritual gifts? *That you not be uninformed.* (Since there is a specific command here, understanding spiritual gifts must be important.)

List and explain the contrasts found in verses 4-6. Hint: Look for the word *but.*

■ Who do you see at work here? *Varieties of gifts—same Spirit; varieties of services—same Lord; varieties of activities—same God. Spirit-Lord-God implies the Trinity at work here.* (It's important to note also that we see varieties—differences—but unity as well. This will come up again.)

■ According to verse 7, who receives the spiritual gifts, and for what purpose? *To each is given . . . for the common good.* (Who is "each?" The clues are in who wrote the letter and to whom it was written. It was written by Paul—a believer—to the church at Corinth—a group of believers.)

■ What do verses 8-11 have to say about the giving of gifts? *They are given by the Spirit as the Spirit chooses.* (Also we see again a variety of gifts being given; and no one individual receives *all* the gifts.)

■ What analogy does Paul use with respect to gifts in verses 12-17? What does this analogy illustrate? Why do you think Paul chose to use it? *The human body. It uses the interdependence of the members of the body to illustrate that even though our spiritual gifts are different, we need each other for the whole church to function well. He probably used this because it was easy to understand.*

- Who determines our place in the body according to verse 18? *God.*
- What do we learn about the individual members of the body from verses 19-24? *All are important. All are indispensable.*
- What is being said in verses 27 about our responsibility toward one another? *There is no room for dissension or jealousy in the body. We are to care for one another.*

- We learned in verses 8-11 that a variety of gifts are given. According to verses 28-30, is there any gift that is received by every member? *No.* (The way these verses are worded in the Greek means the answers to this question is automatically "no.")

Romans 12:1-8

- What principles might Paul be trying to get across in verses 1-3? *There are several good teachings in here: Serving God is an act of worship.* (This one is key for our understanding spiritual gifts.) *Do not be conformed to this world. Be transformed by the renewing of your minds. Think of yourself with sober judgment. God has assigned to each of us a measure of faith.*
- What analogy does Paul reference again in verses 4-5? Why? What is his point? *Again, he uses the human body as an analogy for the church. He is saying that we do not have the same function, but we are one body in Christ.* (There's that diversity with unity thing again!)
- What do we learn about exercising our gifts from verses 6-8? *That our gifts differ according to the grace given us, and we ought to exercise them accordingly; that is, according to the peculiar characteristics of that gift.*

Ephesians 4:1-16

- What is the instruction given in verses 1-3? *Again, there are several: Lead a life worthy of your calling; be humble, gentle, patient, and forbearing with each other; maintain the unity of the Spirit.* (Unity again—hmmm, must be very important!)
- What are the seven characteristics common to all believers according to verses 4-6? What is the significance of this? *One body, one Spirit, one hope, one Lord, one faith, one baptism, one God.* (They may come up with their own interpretations of this. We place a lot of importance sometimes on small differences among Christian practices. In the end, though, we have these seven essential characteristics of the Christian faith in common! We need to focus on the things that unite us, not the things that divide us.)
- Who receives the gifts according to verse 7? *Each of us.*
- For what purpose are gifts given according to verses 11-13? *To equip the saints for the work of ministry, for building up the body of Christ.* (You might ask, "Who are the saints?" The answer is that we are. The word *saints* as used here refer to those who are sanctified through Christ.)
  What are the results in verses 14-16? *The church will grow together in love and not be misled by false teachings.*

1 Peter 4:10-11

- Who receives spiritual gifts? *Each one.*
- How are spiritual gifts to be used? *To serve one another and for the glory of God.*
- What are the two categories of gifts found in this passage? *Speaking and serving.*

Identify the Spiritual Gifts *(10 minutes)*
  Ask participants to go back into their

same small groups. Have them turn to page 8 in their workbook where they will find the chart where they are asked to "List the spiritual gifts you find in each of the Bible passages." Working as groups, ask each group to complete the charts in their workbooks.

A completed chart based on the New Revised Standard Version of the Bible would look like this:

1 Corinthians 12:8-10, 28-30	Romans 12:1-8	Ephesians 4:1-16
Utterance of Wisdom	Prophecy	Apostleship
Utterance of Knowledge	Ministering (Service/Helps)	Prophecy
Faith	Teaching	Evangelism
Gifts of Healing	Exhortation	Pastor-Teacher
Working of Miracles	Generosity (Giving)	
Prophecy	Leading with Diligence	
Discernment of Spirits	Compassion (Mercy)	
Various Kinds of Tongues		
Interpretation of Tongues		
Apostleship		
Teaching		
Assistance (Helps)		
Leadership		

The purpose here is just to see what the Bible identifies as spiritual gifts. Some translations of the Bible may have them worded a little differently, but the essential meaning is the same. Note that in Ephesians 4:11, the way the text is written in Greek makes pastor-teacher one gift, as opposed to listing pastor as one and teacher as another.

Summarize Spiritual Gifts *(10 minutes)*

While you write responses on the white board or newsprint, ask participants quickly to summarize what they have learned about spiritual gifts from Scripture.

Optional Closing Prayer:

As a closing, listen prayerfully to "One Heart," a music selecion on the Leader CD. The Chorus, printed below, is similar to Ephesians 4:6.

One Heart

One heart, one mind, one love is with us all the time.
One life, one light, one spirit in the world tonight.

If you are doing only a 60-minute session, tell participants that their assignment for next time is to read the Introduction and Chapter 1 in their workbook. Tell participants **not** *to work on the Spiritual Gifts Discovery Tool yet; they will be asked to complete that during Session 2. End the session by praying for God to watch over each of the participants as they ponder what they have learned so far.*

If you are doing a 120-minute session, go on to Session 2 in this leader's guide now.

Spiritual Gifts
The Biblical Foundation

Now concerning spiritual gifts, brothers and sisters, I do not want you to be uninformed. —1 Corinthians 12:1

In the Bible passage above, Paul clearly states the importance of the subject of spiritual gifts to Christians. Spiritual gifts and gifts-based ministry are the foundations for understanding how the church is meant to operate, and for understanding our individual roles within the church. In order to understand spiritual gifts, we must examine the context in which they were first given, which begins with Christ's promise to send the Holy Spirit.

As Jesus' earthly ministry was coming to an end, He began to prepare His disciples for the time when they would be called upon to carry on the work He had started. Jesus was returning to God, but He promised the disciples they would not be left alone. The Holy Spirit would come and would teach the disciples all they would need to know in order to continue His ministry.

"Very truly, I tell you, the one who believes in me will also do the works that I do and, in fact, will do greater works than these, because I am going to the Father. I will do whatever you ask in my name, so that the Father may be glorified in the Son. If in my name you ask me for anything, I will do it. If you love me, you will keep my commandments. And I will ask the Father, and he will give you another Advocate, to be with you forever. This is the Spirit of truth, whom the world cannot receive, because it neither sees him nor knows him. You know him, because he abides with you, and he will be in you. I will not leave you orphaned; I am coming to you."

—John 14:12-18

"But the Advocate, the Holy Spirit, whom the Father will send in my name, will teach you everything, and remind you of all that I have said to you."

—John 14:26

"When the Advocate comes, whom I will send to you from the Father, the Spirit of truth who comes from the Father, he will testify on my behalf. You also are to testify because you have been with me from the beginning."

—John 15:26-27

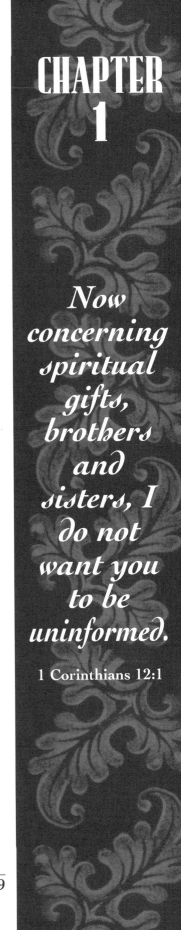

CHAPTER 1

Now concerning spiritual gifts, brothers and sisters, I do not want you to be uninformed.

1 Corinthians 12:1

"When they bring you before the synagogues, the rulers, and the authorities, do not worry about how you are to defend yourselves or what you are to say; for the Holy Spirit will teach you at that very hour what you ought to say."

–Luke 12:11-12

. . .and he said to them, "Thus it is written, that the Messiah is to suffer and to rise from the dead on the third day, and that repentance and forgiveness of sins is to be proclaimed in his name to all nations, beginning from Jerusalem. You are witnesses of these things. And see, I am sending upon you what my Father promised; so stay here in the city until you have been clothed with power from on high."

–Luke 24:46-49.

We don't know at this point exactly what the disciples were thinking or feeling, but it appears they still did not totally understand what Jesus was telling them. His actual departure on what we call Ascension Day must have only added to their confusion and uncertainty. As Jesus ascended, He took the opportunity to address them one last time:

While staying with them, he ordered them not to leave Jerusalem, but to wait there for the promise of the Father. "This," he said, "is what you have heard from me; for John baptized with water, but you will be baptized with the Holy Spirit not many days from now." So when they had come together, they asked him, "Lord, is this the time when you will restore the kingdom to Israel?" He replied, "It is not for you to know the times or periods that the Father has set by his own authority. But you will receive power when the Holy Spirit has come upon you; and you will be my witnesses in Jerusalem, in all Judea and Samaria, and to the ends of the earth."

–Acts 1:4-8

Just as Jesus instructed, the disciples returned to Jerusalem and waited. It was the time of Pentecost, a Jewish harvest festival requiring Jews to gather in Jerusalem for thanksgiving and worship. People came from many different countries, speaking many different languages, to take part in the celebration. At that time, a group of 120 believers in the risen Christ, including the eleven remaining disciples, gathered in one place. Acts 2:1-28 tells of how the promised Holy Spirit came upon these believers, giving them a spiritual gift for speaking in tongues (other languages.) The believers preached in these foreign languages throughout the city that day. Foreigners staying in Jerusalem heard the disciples speaking in their own languages about the mighty works of God. Three thousand people heard God's message and also believed. The church was born.

Followers of Christ received gifts of the Holy Spirit once they accepted Christ as their Savior. References to these spiritual gifts appear throughout the rest of the New Testament. Some believers were given the word of wisdom, some leadership, some the gift of exhortation, and so on. They each served the rest of the community of believers in accordance with their individual gifts, together meeting the needs of all and glorifying God.

Somehow over the ages, this church model in which all Christians used their gifts and shared the work of the church with the Bible as their guide was discarded. Instead, church leaders held most of the power, authority, and responsibility. Many abuses took place as the church fell prey to lust for power and wealth.

The Protestant Reformation, which reached a peak with Martin Luther and John Calvin in the sixteenth century, was built around three core beliefs:

■ The Bible is the final authority.
■ Justification comes through faith and the grace of God, not through human works.
■ All believers are priests.

While the first two brought about change to the church, the third element was not fully realized. The belief in the priesthood of all believers impacted our views regarding our access to God. We don't need an intermediary to go to God on our behalf. We can speak directly to God. However, the implications of the priesthood of all believers were never carried through far enough regarding laypersons and a gift-based ministry. The Reformers talked about the priesthood of all believers and equipping the saints, but these principles were not widely practiced.

Across the world today, there is a movement to bring the church back to a gifts-based ministry model. This is not a new trend or fad; this is restoring God's church to God's perfect plan. By reviving gifts-based ministry, with every believer being a minister, the church is better equipped to achieve the Great Commission of Matthew 28:19, *"Go therefore and make disciples of all nations. . ."* Every spiritual gift is designed to equip us to fulfill the Great Commission. As Christians, we are responsible for carrying on Christ's work. God has given us gifts,

While it is good to turn to the Bible for information, we should also let the Bible form us inside. Open your Bible to 1 Corinthians 13, and take a moment to prepare yourself to be in prayer over the next five minutes or so. Slowly, prayerfully, read 1 Corinthians 13:4-7. Let it be your prayer. Conclude by asking God for help in being more loving in all that you do.

empowering us to serve one another and glorify Him.

Four foundational Bible passages guide us in thinking about spiritual gifts: 1 Corinthians 12; Romans 12:1-8; Ephesians 4:1-16; and 1 Peter 4:10-11. From these four passages we gather much of what we know about spiritual gifts. We've pulled out some key portions of these passages, which set the context for spiritual gifts. Let's stop here and consider what the Bible has to say.

Read each of the listed Bible references and follow the instructions.

1 Corinthians 12
According to verse 1, what is Paul's desire regarding the subject of spiritual gifts?

If you like drawing, try your hand at depicting Paul's use of the human body as an analogy for the variety of spiritual gifts.

List and explain the contrasts found in verses 4-6. Hint: Look for the word *but*. Who do you see at work here?

According to verse 7, who receives the spiritual gifts, and for what purpose?

List the spiritual gifts you find in each of the Bible passages:

1 Corinthians 12:8-10, 28-30	Romans 12:1-8	Ephesians 4:1-16

What do verses 8-11 have to say about the giving of gifts?

We learned in verses 8-11 that a variety of gifts are given. According to verses 28-30, is there any gift that is received by every member?

What analogy does Paul use with respect to gifts in verses 12-17? What does this analogy illustrate? Why do you think Paul chose to use it?

Romans 12:1-8
What principles might Paul be trying to get across in verses 1-3?

Who determines our place in the body of Christ according to verse 18?

What analogy does Paul reference again in verses 4-5? Why? What's his point?

What do we learn about the individual members of the body from verses 19-24?

What do we learn about exercising our gifts from verses 6-8?

What is being said in verses 25-27 about our responsibility toward one another?

Ephesians 4:1-16
What is the instruction given in verses 1-3?

What are the seven characteristics common to all believers according to verses 4-6? What is the significance of this?

1 Peter 4:10-11

Who receives spiritual gifts?

Who receives the gifts according to verse 7?

How are spiritual gifts to be used?

For what purpose are gifts given according to verses 11-13?

What are the two categories of gifts found in this passage?

What are the results in verses 14-16?

Well, we've learned a lot today about the broad biblical context for spiritual gifts. The focus now turns to us as unique individuals. It's time to start the process of discovering the particular gifts God has given to each one of us.

SESSION 2
SPIRITUAL GIFTS DISCOVERY

If you are doing four 120-minute sessions, you will pick up here immediately following the end of Session 1. You will probably wish to take a 10-minute break before starting in on the material contained here in Session 2.

If you are doing eight 60-minute sessions, Session 2 is a separate, stand-alone session.

OBJECTIVE FOR THIS SESSION:

To take the Spiritual Gifts Discovery Tool and to debrief its results.

Prepare by reading in advance the material in Session 2 in the leader's guide. Be sure to take the Spiritual Gifts Discovery Tool yourself. Read Kingdom, Church, and personal benefits of understanding your gifts.

If you are using the overhead slides, either print the overheads for Session 2 for use on a projector or bring the disk for use with a computer and projector. Make extra copies of the Spiritual Gifts Discovery Tool in case a participant does not bring his or her book. You may want to listen to the four musical selections on the CD-ROM to select a couple for use as the group takes their gifts assessment or as an ending prayer.

Materials Needed: pens or pencils; white board or newsprint with appropriate markers; Bibles; workbooks; several handheld calculators.

Welcome and Pray *(5 minutes)*

Welcome participants back and open with prayer asking for God to open the minds and hearts of the people present so that all of you might be prepared to hear what God wants to say to you.

Benefits of Discovering Your Gifts *(5 minutes)*

Briefly present the benefits for Kingdom, Church and personal benefits of discovering, developing and using your spiritual gifts from the Student Book, end of Chapter 2.

Take the Spiritual Gifts Discovery Tool *(20 minutes)*

Tell participants to turn to page 11 in their workbook, to the instructions and the first page of the Spiritual Gifts Discovery Tool. Note that they are to place a number "0" through "4," based on the key at the start of the tool, to the left of each statement. Emphasize that they are to answer based on how true these statements are of their actual life experience, both past and present—not as they wish they were. When they get to the end of the 80 statements, then they need to transfer all of their numbers to the Response Form on page 15. When they are done with that, they should check to make sure that all their numbers are transferred correctly and then wait for your instructions. They will have twenty minutes.

Start them with this prayer: Gracious God, send your Holy Spirit to guide your people so that they might truly learn what their spiritual gifts are so that they may use them to your glory. In Jesus' name we pray. Amen. (If you wish, play some quiet instrumental music in the background, such as the music tracks *New Hope* or *Who Do You Say I Am?* from the Leader CD.)

Score the Spiritual Gifts Discovery Tool (10 minutes)

If someone is having difficulty transferring their numbers to the Spiritual Gifts Discovery Tool Response Form on page 15, you or someone else might need to help them. When everyone is ready, ask participants to add each line across. Distribute handheld calculators to those who wish to use them.

Because not everyone is comfortable with arithmetic or with filling out forms, be ready to help persons who are unsure that they are doing things right—or ask other participants to help their neighbors.

When everyone has completed the response form, have participants transfer their totals to the Spiritual Gifts Discovery Tool Answer Key on page 15. Then ask them to circle their three highest numerical scores. They should then write the corresponding spiritual gifts in the box labeled "My top three gifts according to my scores." Persons with ties for third highest may at least temporarily have more than three gifts listed.

Note that participants should also mark yes or no for spiritual gifts Q, R, and S. They are "self-evident" in that when the Holy Spirit chooses to work them in and through you, you know it!

Encourage participants to focus on their highest scores regardless of what the scores are. Some people score themselves more conservatively than others. There is no threshold or minimum to be reached.

Debrief Spiritual Gifts Discovery Tool Results (20 minutes)

Divide the larger group into small groups of three participants each. Announce that each person will have five minutes during which the focus will be on their results from the Spiritual Gifts Discovery Tool. They should at least share what their top three gifts were according to their scores, but then they can use the remainder of the five minutes as they wish. They might share surprise or puzzlement about the results. They might look for confirmation from the other two participants. They might ask how the other two understand those spiritual gifts. When the five minutes are up, though, you as leader will let the large group know and the focus will shift to another person in each of the small groups. You will do this for a total of three periods so that each participant will have an opportunity to have the focus on their results within their small group.

Whether you are doing a 60-minute session or a 120-session, you are now at the end of the session.

Whether this has been a 60-minute or a 120-minute session, tell the participants that their assignment for the next time is to review the lengthy material in Chapter 2. If their small groups missed working on any of the Bible study in Chapter 2, they should complete it. If this has been a 120-minute session, tell participants that for next time they need to read Chapters 3 and 4 on "Talents" and "Resources" as well, and answer any questions they find there.

Close the session with prayer asking God to watch over all the participants, blessing them with increasing clarity about their spiritual gifts.

Spiritual Gifts Discovery Tool

The following is a list of 80 statements. Before considering these, make sure you have set aside an uninterrupted time of quiet. Begin this time with prayer, and ask the Holy Spirit to guide you. Answer based on how true these statements are of your life experience, both past and present, not as you wish you would be. Remember, God's choice of gifts for you is in harmony with His perfect plan and will for your life.

Record your answers on the line next to each statement. When you are finished, transfer your responses onto the response form. Score each one as follows:

4. Very true of me, consistently.
3. Frequently true of me.
2. Occasionally true of me.
1. Infrequently true of me.
0. Rarely, or never true of me.

_____1. I am organized and detail-oriented.

_____2. I would enjoy starting a church in a foreign country or culture.

_____3. I can sense when someone's motives or intentions are inconsistent with the teachings of Scripture.

_____4. I encourage people who are struggling in their faith through speaking, writing, artwork, singing, or prayer.

_____5. I am open about my faith, and look for opportunities to talk about it.

_____6. I am confident that God will keep His promises.

_____7. I enjoy sharing my material blessings with others.

_____8. From time-to-time, my prayers for healing on behalf of others are answered in miraculous ways.

_____9. I find fulfillment through performing behind-the-scenes deeds that support ministries.

_____10. I enjoy studying my Bible in depth.

_____11. People often come to me for direction.

_____12. My heart goes out to people who are hurting, and I am moved to action.

_____13. I am concerned about the spiritual growth of people I know.

_____14. I confront individuals and groups who have wandered, and encourage them to turn back to God.

_____15. I am able to explain Biblical teachings in ways that others can relate to their lives.

_____16. People often ask me for insight and guidance on difficult decisions or situations.

_____17. I enjoy planning and organizing events or projects.

_____18. I am skilled at overseeing many projects at once.

_____19. I know when a statement or doctrine is not in line with God's word.

_____20. I am able to gently influence people in a way that helps them remain faithful.

_____21. I often invite people to come to church with me.

_____22. I don't get discouraged when bad things happen, because I know God is in control.

_____23. I have ample income, and give a significant portion to charitable causes.

_____24. The Holy Spirit prompts me to pray for specific people who are in need and are hurting.

_____25. I enjoy using my talents and skills to help various ministries.

_____26. When someone is confused, I am able to point out a Scripture passage that leads them to the truth.

_____27. I provide inspiration in the work of ministry and support others to accomplish the ministry's goals.

_____28. I desire to follow the example of Jesus, reaching out to people in need with compassion.

_____29. Sometimes I develop relationships with others and nurture them in their faith walk.

_____30. I see things in society that are opposed to God's will, and feel led to expose them.

_____31. I enjoy preparing and organizing material in order to teach it to others.

_____32. The solutions I provide to complex situations are always consistent with Biblical truth as found in Scripture.

_____33. I easily outline and implement the steps needed to achieve a vision.

_____34. I like to empower others to assume leadership roles.

_____35. I have been able to call the focus of individuals and groups back to the Holy Spirit and God's word.

_____36. I bring comfort to people through sharing God's promises.

_____37. I can share the gospel in relevant, meaningful ways.

_____38. I am able to provide reassurance and encouragement to individuals or groups when they are thinking of giving up.

_____ 39. When I see someone in need, I will share whatever I have with him.

_____ 40. I believe that God answers my prayers for miraculous healings.

_____ 41. I often help out around the church by doing "whatever needs to be done."

_____ 42. I like to share with others what I have learned through studying the Bible.

_____ 43. I encourage others to develop their skills and abilities.

_____ 44. I enjoy visiting people who are sick or lonely to bring them a little cheer.

_____ 45. I enjoy teaching individuals and groups over extended periods of time.

_____ 46. The Holy Spirit urges me to speak forth the mind and counsel of God in order to encourage or guide people.

_____ 47. Whenever I learn something new, I am thinking about how I might share the new knowledge with others.

_____ 48. I sometimes bring clarity to difficult situations and can help point others toward God's will.

_____ 49. I am skilled at gathering and managing the resources needed for a ministry in order for it function properly.

_____ 50. I am drawn to proclaim and teach the gospel in places where it has not been heard or taught.

_____ 51. I sometimes sense the presence of evil.

_____ 52. People are motivated to make Godly decisions or changes in their lives after spending time with me.

_____ 53. I intentionally develop relationships with non-Christians for the purpose of sharing my faith.

_____ 54. I believe God listens to and answers all prayers.

_____ 55. I believe I have been blessed with abundant resources so that I can be a blessing to others.

_____ 56. I am drawn to worship experiences where prayers and anointing for healing are experienced.

_____ 57. I enjoy providing practical assistance to meet ministry needs.

_____ 58. I am able to speak and teach an understanding of God and the Bible that helps others grow in faith.

_____ 59. I often find myself in a leadership role.

_____ 60. I am a good listener, and people often talk to me about their troubles.

_____ 61. I feel the responsibility of caring for the people I teach about God and His word.

_____ 62. I am often led to convict people of wrong and to help them get back on the Godly path.

_____ 63. People often thank me for helping them to better understand the Bible or materials from a Bible study.

_____ 64. I am able to share words and insights that bring peaceful solutions to problems.

_____ 65. I like to work with issues involving systems, structure and procedures.

_____ 66. I feel compelled to share the gospel, and spend time in prayer and God's word to prepare myself.

_____ 67. I have experienced, personally and in groups, guidance from the Holy Spirit in answer to a time of prayer.

_____ 68. I am led to encourage people in their faith through action.

_____ 69. I am comfortable using prayer and Scripture to lead people to Christ.

_____ 70. I approach challenges with confidence when I know I am following the will of God.

_____ 71. Everything I have is a gift from God and I seek out ways to share those gifts with others.

_____ 72. People have shared tangible ways in which they have experienced God's healing touch as a result of my prayers on their behalf.

_____ 73. Serving God through simple tasks is something I find rewarding.

_____ 74. God sometimes gives me a special insight into His word that enables me to teach others in a way that helps them understand.

_____ 75. I tend to have a "big picture" perspective and can clearly communicate vision in a way that is understandable and motivating.

_____ 76. I can minister to people in need in a way that protects their dignity.

_____ 77. I am not only interested in instructing people about God, but also care about their restoration and relationship with God.

_____ 78. God's word and /or will sometimes come to mind in situations where people need conviction or encouragement.

_____ 79. I look for opportunities to share what I have learned about the Bible.

_____80. The Holy Spirit provides me with spiritual thoughts and words to share to help bring focus and clarity in times of disorder.

Place your responses to the statements in the appropriate box below.

4—Very true of me, consistently.
3—Frequently true of me.
2—Occasionally true of me.
1—Infrequently true of me.
0—Rarely, or never true of me.

Total your responses across. **TOTAL**

1___ 17___ 33___ 49___ 65___ A_____
2___ 18___ 34___ 50___ 66___ B_____
3___ 19___ 35___ 51___ 67___ C_____
4___ 20___ 36___ 52___ 68___ D_____
5___ 21___ 37___ 53___ 69___ E_____
6___ 22___ 38___ 54___ 70___ F_____
7___ 23___ 39___ 55___ 71___ G_____
8___ 24___ 40___ 56___ 72___ H_____
9___ 25___ 41___ 57___ 73___ I_____
10___ 26___ 42___ 58___ 74___ J_____
11___ 27___ 43___ 59___ 75___ K_____
12___ 28___ 44___ 60___ 76___ L_____
13___ 29___ 45___ 61___ 77___ M_____
14___ 30___ 46___ 62___ 78___ N_____
15___ 31___ 47___ 63___ 79___ O_____
16___ 32___ 48___ 64___ 80___ P_____

Spiritual Gifts	Total Score
A. Administration/Leadership	_____
B. Apostleship	_____
C. Discernment of Spirits	_____
D. Exhortation (Encouragement)	_____
E. Evangelism	_____
F. Faith	_____
G. Generosity	_____
H. Healing	_____
I. Assistance/Helps	_____
J. Utterance of Knowledge	_____
K. Leadership/Leading with Diligence	_____
L. Mercy/Compassion	_____
M. Pastor-Teacher (Shepherding)	_____
N. Prophecy	_____
O. Teaching	_____
P. Utterance of Wisdom	_____

Please mark yes/no whether you have these self-evident spiritual gifts:

Q. Miracles . . . . ❑Yes ❑No
R. Tongues. . . . . ❑Yes ❑No
S. Interpretation of Tongues . . . ❑Yes ❑No

My top three gifts, according to my scores, are:

1. _____

2. _____

3. _____

SESSION 3
SPIRITUAL GIFTS DEFINED

OBJECTIVE FOR THIS SESSION:

To further understand the biblical foundation of spiritual gifts with the goal of gaining an appreciation for how they manifest themselves today.

Prepare by reading in advance the material in the Chapter 2 in the workbook, and in Session 2 in the leader's guide. Read all Bible passages for yourself. Try all instructions given both in the workbook and the leader's guide.

Watch the CD-ROM video segment, "Chapters 2-3, Gifts and Talents." If you are using the overhead slides, either print the overheads for Session 2 for use on a projector or bring the disk to use with a computer and projector.

Materials Needed: blank nametags (if participants might still be unfamiliar with one another); pens or pencils; white board or newsprint with appropriate markers; Bibles; workbooks

If You Are Starting a 60-Minute Session... *(10 minutes)*
Welcome participants back and open with prayer asking for God to send the Holy Spirit upon those gathered to help in understanding the gifts God gives in order to build up the Church and to spread the good news of the love of God made known to us through Jesus Christ.

Ask if there are any questions about the material covered last session. Take a few minutes to review what they learned about spiritual gifts last time. Have participants call out what they learned, and write it on the white board or newsprint. Check the summary the group made last time to make sure nothing important was missed.

Work Through the Definitions and Uses of Spiritual Gifts *(40 minutes)*
Ask participants to form *different* small groups than they were in previously, again with three to five members in each group. Draw their attention to the lengthy section in Chapter 2 of their workbook on pages 19 to 28, where they will find the definitions of the nineteen spiritual gifts mentioned in the Bible. As groups, their tasks are:

■ To read through the definition of each spiritual gift. (They do not have to read through each biblical reference unless they feel it would help their understanding—they will not have time to read all of the Bible passages listed during the time allotted for this learning activity.)
■ To come to an understanding of what each spiritual gift might look like and how it might be used within the church today.
■ To discuss whether anyone in the group knows of anyone else inside or outside of the congregation whom they think might have that particular spiritual gift and how they might be encouraged in their exercise of it.

Each small group should work their way

as far through the nineteen biblical spiritual gifts as time allows. You might want to stagger where the small groups begin in the list so that all the spiritual gifts are covered by a group.

Summarize

After bringing the groups back together, report on what each gift might look like in the church today.

If you are doing a 60-minute session, tell participants that their assignment for next time is to read Chapters 3 and 4. They should also follow the instructions on page 29 of the workbook to list and research what the Bible says about the three gifts on which they received the highest scores. If you are doing a 120-minute session, go on to Session 4 in this leader's guide now.

Spiritual Gifts Defined

Like good stewards of the manifold grace of God, serve one another with whatever gift each of you has received. —1 Peter 4:10

Let's talk for a moment about the definition of spiritual gifts. . .

> **Spiritual gifts are special (divine) abilities given to every Christian, by the grace of God, through the Holy Spirit, to be used to serve and strengthen one another, and to glorify God.**

So, in a nutshell, spiritual gifts are:
- Divine abilities (not something you've learned)
- Given to every Christian (yes, even YOU)
- Given through the grace of God (not something you've earned)
- Given by the Holy Spirit (He chooses which gift(s) you receive)
- Used to serve and strengthen one another (to build each other up, not yourself)
- Used to glorify God (for God's purposes, to God's glory)

By now, you should have prayerfully considered the questions within the spiritual gifts discovery tool and possibly identified your top three spiritual gifts. Written assessments are meant to be helpful tools that assist you in narrowing down the possibilities and allowing you to focus on a few of the nineteen spiritual gifts we enumerate here. Confirmation that you have a certain spiritual gift may come in a variety of ways:
- You will be drawn to use your spiritual gift(s). (You are drawn to do what God has equipped you to do.)
- Others will recognize that gift in you. (Others are benefiting).
- You will be comfortable serving in your area of spiritual giftedness. (This doesn't mean you won't have butterflies!)
- You will be effective when you exercise that gift. (God gets the glory.)

Take a deep breath. It's time to continue our journey! We are really blazing trails now! Our path is leading us to a deeper understanding of each of the spiritual gifts. If you have time, look up the Bible reference noted with each spiritual gift. The Bible is rich with truth for us. The Holy Spirit is our teacher and our guide to understanding what God wants us to know.

In the section that follows, we've provided a list of nineteen spiritual gifts referred to in the Bible. A transliteration of the Greek word used in

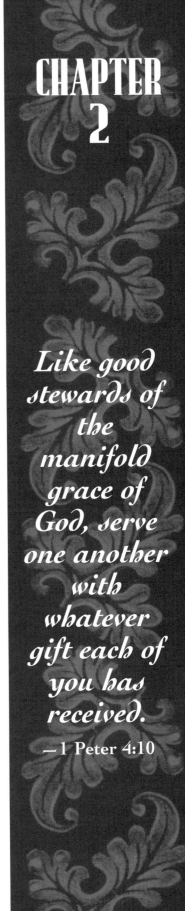

Like good stewards of the manifold grace of God, serve one another with whatever gift each of you has received.

—1 Peter 4:10

the New Testament for the spiritual gift is given, followed by a definition. Then we offer our best understanding of the spiritual gift. Bible references to each spiritual gift is given, followed by space for you to reflect on where and how you see each specific spiritual gift around you or within you today.

Apostleship

Greek: apŏstŏlŏs = a delegate, a special ambassador of the Gospel, officially a commissioner of Christ, a messenger, one who is sent

The divine ability to build the foundation of new churches by preaching the Word, teaching others to live by Christ's commandments through the example of their own lives, and preparing the people to serve one another. Persons with this gift are eager to bring the Gospel to those who have never heard it. They enthusiastically approach new ministries, churches, or settings, and realize the need to adapt methods of evangelism and service to widely different environments. People with this gift envision themselves as missionaries, or they may accept and exercise leadership over a number of new churches.

Scripture References: Ephesians 4:11-13; Acts 6:2-4; 2 Peter 3:2; 1 Thessalonians 2:6

Examples of use today:

Do you know anyone who has the gift of Apostleship?

How can you encourage them as they exercise their spiritual gift?

Do you believe you have the spiritual gift of Apostleship?

Assistance/Helps

Greek: diakŏnia = attendance, aid, relief, service, ministry

The God-given ability to work alongside others in performing practical and often behind-the-scenes tasks to sustain and enhance the Body of Christ. A person with this gift receives spiritual satisfaction from doing everyday necessary tasks; he or she may prefer to work quietly and without public recognition. When a need is seen, the helper frequently takes care of it without being asked. The helper's work often frees up other persons so that they may carry out their own ministries.

Scripture References: Hebrews 6:10; Acts 24:23; 2 Timothy 4:11; Philippians 2:25-30

Examples of use today:

Do you know anyone who has the gift of Assistance?

How can you encourage them as they exercise their spiritual gift?

Do you believe you have the spiritual gift of Assistance? Why?

Discernment of Spirits

Greek: διακρισις = judicial estimation, discerning
pnĕuma = a current of air, figuratively "a spirit," mental disposition

The divine ability to recognize what is of God and what is not of God—to distinguish between good and evil, truth and error, and pure motives and impure motives. People with this gift usually can rely on instincts or first impressions to tell when a person or message is deceptive or inconsistent with biblical truths. They can sense the presence of evil, and question motives, intentions, doctrine, deeds, and beliefs. These people must take care to use their gift in a way that brings good to the Body of Christ—to judge with mercy and understanding rather than to condemn.

Scripture References: 1 John 4:1; Acts 13:8-12; 2 Corinthians 11:13-15; Acts 17:11

Examples of use today:

Do you know anyone who has the gift of Discernment of Spirits?

How can you encourage them as they exercise their spiritual gift?

Do you believe you have the spiritual gift of Discernment of Spirits? Why?

Evangelism

Greek: ĕuaggĕlistēs = a preacher of the Gospel

The divine ability to spread the Good News of Jesus Christ so that unknowing persons respond with faith and discipleship. People with this gift speak comfortably about their faith; nonbelievers are drawn into this circle of comfort. These people enjoy many friendships outside of their Christian community. They enjoy helping others see how Christianity can fulfill their needs. They eagerly study questions that challenge Christianity. They respond clearly in ways that connect with individuals.

Scripture References: Acts 5:42; Luke 9:6; Acts 16:6-10; Acts 8:26-40

Examples of use today:

Do you know anyone who has the gift of Evangelism?

How can you encourage them as they exercise their spiritual gift?

Do you believe you have the spiritual gift of Evangelism?
Why?

Exhortation

Greek: paraklēsis = imploration, solace, comfort, exhortation, entreaty

The God-given ability to encourage, help, intercede for, and be an advocate for others in a way that motivates others to grow in their faith and urges them to action. Exhortation takes many forms, and can be done through personal relationships, music, writings, intercessory prayer, and speaking to name a few. People with this gift encourage others to remain faithful, even in the midst of struggles. They are sensitive and sympathetic toward another person's emotional state, and exhort selflessly, with affection, not contempt. They can see positive traits or aspects that other persons overlook, and often have more faith in other persons than they have in themselves.

Scripture References: Acts 14:22; Acts 20:1-2; Acts 15:31-33; 2 Timothy 4:2

Examples of use today:

Do you know anyone who has the gift of Exhortation?

How can you encourage them as they exercise their spiritual gift?

Do you believe you have the spiritual gift of Exhortation? Why?

Faith

Greek: pistis = faith in God, a personal surrender to God with a conduct inspired by such surrender; moral conviction, assurance

The divine ability to recognize what God wants done and to act when others fall back in doubt. Even in the face of barriers that overwhelm others, people with this gift simply know that God will see it done. Believing deeply in the power of prayer, they also know that God is both present and active in their lives. People with this gift, by their works and by their words, show others that God is faithful to God's promises.

Scripture References: Ephesians 2:8-9; 1 Timothy 6:11; Acts 14:22; Matthew 9:2, 22

Examples of use today:

Do you know anyone who has the gift of Faith?

How can you encourage them as they exercise their spiritual gift?

Do you believe you have the spiritual gift of Faith? Why?

Greek: mĕtaдiдōmi = to give over, share, impart

The God-given ability to give material wealth freely and joyfully, knowing that spiritual wealth will abound as God's work is advanced. People with this gift usually manage their finances well, may have a special ability to make money, and tend to be frugal in their lifestyle. They use these skills to increase their support for God's work, and trust that God will provide for their needs. They are often comfortable and successful in approaching others for contributions. Instead of asking, "How much of my money do I give to God?" they ask, "How much of God's money do I keep?"

Scripture References: Luke 3:11; Romans 12:8; 1 Thessalonians 2:8

Examples of use today:

Do you know anyone who has the gift of Generosity?

How can you encourage them as they exercise their spiritual gift?

Do you believe you have the spiritual gift of Generosity? Why?

Greek: charisma a spiritual endowment, a divine gratuity, a religious qualification
iama - cures, healings

The divine ability to bring wholeness—physical, emotional or spiritual—to others. People with this gift listen skillfully as they seek God's guidance to learn the needs of the sick and to determine the causes and nature of an illness. They believe that God can cure and that prayer can overcome any negative forces at work. (They also know that God might have a different agenda.) Their tools include prayer, touch and spoken words. This gift shows God's power; at the same time, it is to His glory. The goal of healing in the New Testament is not healing itself, but spreading the gospel by pointing to the power of Jesus Christ, and to show the glory of God.

Scripture References: Matthew 4:23, Luke 9:11, Acts 10:38, Acts 4:28-30

Examples of use today:

Do you know anyone who has the gifts of Healings?

How can you encourage them as they exercise their spiritual gift?

Do you believe you have the spiritual gifts of Healings? Why?

Interpretation of Tongues

Greek: hermēneia = translation
glōssa = tongues, a language,
specifically one not naturally
learned

The divine ability to translate the message of someone speaking in tongues. People with this gift enable the gift of tongues to build up the church, by interpreting God's message for the people.

Scripture References: 1 Corinthians 12:10; 14

Examples of use today:

Do you know anyone who has the gift of Interpretation of Tongues?

How can you encourage them as they exercise their spiritual gift?

Do you believe you have the spiritual gift of Interpretation of Tongues? Why?

Leadership/Administration

Greek: kubĕrnēsis = pilotage, to steer, a
guide, directorship in the church

The spiritual gift of administration or leadership is the God-given ability to organize and manage information, people, events and resources to accomplish the objectives of a ministry. People with this gift handle details carefully and thoroughly. They are skilled in determining priorities, and in planning and directing the steps needed to achieve a goal. They feel frustrated when faced with disorder, and are uncomfortable with inefficiency.

Scripture References: 1 Corinthians 12:28; Acts 6:1-7; Titus 1:5

Examples of use today:

Do you know anyone who has the gift of Administration?

How can you encourage them as they exercise their spiritual gift?

Do you believe you have the spiritual gift of Administration? Why?

Greek: prŏŭstēmi = to stand before, to preside, maintain, be over

The divine ability to motivate, coordinate, and direct people doing God's work. People with this gift are visionaries who inspire others to work together to make the vision a reality. They take responsibility for setting and achieving goals; they step in where there is a lack of direction. They build a team of talented persons. Then they empower them. These persons are called to be servant-leaders. Held to a high moral standard, they lead by the example of their own lives.

Scripture References: Philippians 3:17-21; John 13:12-17; Hebrews 13:7, 17

Examples of use today:

Do you know anyone who has the gift of Leading?

How can you encourage them as they exercise their spiritual gift?

Do you believe you have the spiritual gift of Leading? Why?

Greek elĕĕo = to have compassion, to have mercy on

The God-given ability to see and feel the suffering of others and to minister to them with love and understanding. More simply, this gift is compassion, moved to action. People with this gift are called to reach out to someone who is hurt or rejected, easing the suffering. They feel fulfilled when they can show others that God loves them. They are skilled at gaining the trust of those in need and enjoy finding ways to comfort them.

Scripture References: Matthew 9:36; Luke 10:30-37; Colossians 3:12-15

Examples of use today:

Do you know anyone who has the gift of Mercy?

How can you encourage them as they exercise their spiritual gift?

Do you believe you have the spiritual gift of Mercy? Why?

Effecting of Miracles

Greek: ĕnĕrgēma = an effect, working, operation
dunamis = force, power, specifically miraculous power

The divine ability to perform miracles that testify to the truth of the Gospel. People with this gift perform miracles among the people for the purpose of getting their attention, so as to point to the mighty works of God, testifying to the validity of the message being spoken. The performance of these miracles leads to listening, following, and believing in the message by those who witness them.

Scripture Reference: John 2:11; 6:2; Acts 2:22; 8:6, 13; Hebrews 2:4

Examples of use today:

Do you know anyone who has the gift of Effecting of Miracles?

How can you encourage them as they exercise their spiritual gift?

Do you believe you have the spiritual gift of Effecting of Miracles? Why?

Pastor-Teacher

Greek: pŏimēn = a shepherd
didaskalŏs = an instructor, master, teacher

The divine ability to guide, protect, and care for other Christians as they experience spiritual growth. People with this gift enjoy working with groups of people and nurturing their growth over an extended period of time. Because of these long-term relationships, they establish trust and confidence, and are able to take the time to care for the "whole person." They can assess where a person is spiritually, and then develop or find places where that person can continue a journey of faith. They model compassion.

Scripture References: 1 Peter 5:1-4; John 10:1-16; Jeremiah 3:15; 17:16; Ezekiel 34; Ephesians 4:11-16

Examples of use today:

Do you know anyone who has the gift of Pastor-Teacher?

How can you encourage them as they exercise their spiritual gift?

Do you believe you have the spiritual gift of Pastor-Teacher? Why?

Prophecy

Greek: prophēteuō = speak under inspiration, speak forth the mind and counsel of God

The God-given ability to proclaim God's truth in a way that makes it relevant to current situations and to envision how God would want things to change. The goal may be to bring about repentance, correction, or enlightenment. People with this gift listen carefully to God for what God wants them to say. They warn people of the immediate or future consequences of not accepting God's truths. They see sin or deception that others overlook. Prophets speak to the people, bringing edification, exhortation, and consolation.

Scripture Reference: Ephesians 4:11-13; Revelation 19:10; 1 Corinthians 13:2; 14:3

Examples of Use Today:

Do you know anyone who has the gift of Prophecy?

How can you encourage them as they exercise their spiritual gift?

Do you believe you have the spiritual gift of Prophecy? Why?

Teaching

Greek: didaskalia = instruction, the act of imparting the truth

The divine ability to understand and clearly explain God's truths, and to show how we can apply these in our lives. People with this gift enjoy studying the Bible and inspire listeners to greater obedience to God's word. They prepare through study and reflection, and pay close attention to detail. In addition to communicating facts, they are careful to show that the Scriptures have practical applications. They can adapt their presentation in order to communicate God's message to a particular audience effectively.

Scripture References: Matthew 28:19-20; Colossians 1:28; James 3:1; 1 Timothy 6:3-5; Titus 1:7-11

Examples of use today:

Do you know anyone who has the gift of Teaching?

How can you encourage them as they exercise their spiritual gift?

Do you believe you have the spiritual gift of Teaching? Why?

Tongues

Greek: glōssa = tongues, a language, specifically one not naturally learned

The divine ability to speak a message from God to the people in a language one has not naturally learned. The gift of tongues is a sign to unbelievers showing the power and glory of God. There seems to be three types of tongues: speaking in a language the speaker does not know, but the listener does; speaking in a language neither the speaker nor the listeners understand, which requires an interpreter; and a private prayer language. The first two build up the Body of Christ. The third edifies only the speaker, who should not use it in church but only practice it in private.

Scripture Reference: Acts 2:11; 1 Corinthians 14

Examples of use today:

Do you know anyone who has the gift of Tongues?

How can you encourage them as they exercise their spiritual gift?

Do you believe you have the spiritual gift of Tongues? Why?

Utterance of Knowledge/ Word of Knowledge

Greek: lŏgŏs = something said, utterance, communication

gnōsis = knowledge

The God-given ability to understand, organize, and effectively use information to advance God's purposes. The information may come either from the Holy Spirit or from sources around us. People with this gift enjoy studying the Bible and other sources to gain facts, insights, and truths. They use this information for projects, ministries, or teaching. They organize it in order to pass it to other persons for their use and benefit. The Holy Spirit appears to be at work when these people show unusual insight or understanding.

Scripture References: Proverbs 1:7; Jeremiah 3:15; Malachi 2:7, 2; 2 Peter 1:2-11; Romans 10:2-3

Examples of use today:

Do you know anyone who has the gift of Utterance or Word of Knowledge?

How can you encourage them as they exercise their spiritual gift?

Do you believe you have the spiritual gift of Utterance or Word of Knowledge? Why?

Utterance of Wisdom/ Word of Wisdom

Greek: lŏgŏs = something said, utterance, communication
sŏphia = wisdom, higher or lower, earthly or spiritual

The God-given ability to understand and apply biblical and spiritual knowledge to complex, contradictory, or other difficult situations. People with the gift of Word of Wisdom have an ability to understand and live God's will. They share their wisdom with others through teaching and admonition. People with this gift speak God's truth as found in Scripture, in order to provide clarity and direction to people who are struggling with which way they should go. They make practical application of biblical truths. They are, in effect, a "compass" for the Body of Christ.

Scripture References: Colossians 1:9-12, 28; 2:3; 3:16; James 3:13

Examples of use today:

Do you know anyone who has the gift of Utterance or Word of Wisdom?

How can you encourage them as they exercise their spiritual gift?

Do you believe you have the spiritual gift of Utterance or Word of Wisdom? Why?

Many books have been written about spiritual gifts. They can be contradictory and confusing. Make sure you judge the validity of what they say against the Bible. After all, God's word is our "plumb line."

Take time to research what the Bible says about the three gifts on which you received the highest scores. List the gifts in the blanks provided on these pages. Look up the Bible passages listed in this chapter for those gifts, and write down notes and reflections that you find significant.

1.

2.

3.

Let's close this leg of your journey by contemplating the benefits of discovering, developing, and using your spiritual gifts.

KINGDOM BENEFITS:

Above all, God is glorified and God's people are built up in the church as gift-based ministries are taught and developed.

CHURCH BENEFITS

Churches that teach and develop gifts-based ministries are more effective in the ministries they provide. Churches with gifts-based ministries have people with the gift of Leadership leading, people with the gift of Helps helping, people with the gift of Mercy reaching out to persons who are suffering, and so on.

Churches that teach and develop gifts-based ministries grow spiritually. When you use your gifts in service to others, you see God at work through yourself, changing lives and changing the world—one person at a time.

PERSONAL BENEFITS

- *You will have a better understanding of God's purpose for your life.* God gives each person unique gifts to fulfill God's specific plan.
- *Your relationship with God will grow and mature.* As you minister to others and see the difference God makes in their lives through you, your relationship with God will deepen.
- *Your ministry will be more effective and fulfilling.* For example, if you have a passion for children and the gift of Teaching, you will probably be a very effective children's Sunday school teacher. Doing it will energize you!

Notes/Reflections/Questions about Spiritual Gifts:

SESSION 4
TALENTS AND RESOURCES

OBJECTIVE FOR THIS SESSION:

To gain an understanding of talents as distinguished from spiritual gifts; and to see how your resources can affect your ministry within the church.

If you are doing four 120-minute sessions, you will pick up here immediately following the end of Session 3. You will probably wish to take a 5-minute break before starting in on the material contained here in Session 4.

If you are doing eight 60-minute sessions, Session 4 is a separate, stand-alone session.

Prepare by reading in advance the material in Chapter 3 and Chapter 4 in the workbook, and in Session 4 in the leader's guide. Read all Bible passages for yourself. Try all instructions given both in the workbook and the leader's guide.

Watch the CD-ROM video segment, "Chapter 4, Resources." If you are using the overhead slides, either print the overheads for Session 4 for use on a projector or bring the disk for use with a computer and projector.

Materials Needed: blank paper; pens or pencils; white board or newsprint with appropriate markers; Bibles; workbooks

If You Are Starting a 60-Minute Session *(5 minutes)*

Welcome participants back and open with prayer asking for God to nurture the gifts and talents given to the unique individuals gathered in this place that they might serve to build up the Body of Christ and lead more people to Christ's love.

Distinguish Talents from Spiritual Gifts *(10 minutes)*

Review the list of persons on page 31 in the workbook and what their talents are. Possible answers might include:

Michael Jordan: playing basketball, mentoring younger basketball players

Barbra Streisand: singing, acting

Bill Gates: computer programming, entrepreneurship;

Maya Angelou: writing poetry.

Discuss the differences between talents and spiritual gifts. Talents and gifts can be very similar and even overlap, but there are some key differences:

Spiritual Gifts	Talents
Received by every Christian	Received by every human
Beyond natural ability	Natural ability
Always used to serve others and to glorify God	May be used to serve others and to glorify God, but can also be used for own purposes

Your class may come up with others. Acquired abilities are those skills we gain through training or experience. Some examples are: public speaking; facilitation skills; accounting skills; computer skills.

Begin to Identify Talents *(10 minutes)*

Ask participants to brainstorm what talents or acquired skills they think they might have that could be used in serve to Christ.

Write those down on the white board or newsprint. Talk as a group in a general discussion about how they might be nurtured and offered in service through the church.

Introduce the Concept of Resources
(10 minutes)

Most of us think of financial resources when we talk about using our resources to serve others through the Body of Christ. Our resources, though, include our time, our material possessions, our contacts, and our hobbies. Ask participants to identify what they have in their own lives that might be considered resources.

Remind participants of the Parable of the Talents from Matthew 25:14-30, which is reprinted on page 33-34 of the workbook. The parable tells us that we shall be held accountable for the resources we hold. We need to remember that we don't own our resources—they are from God and belong to God; we are stewards entrusted with them by God.

Ask someone to read Matthew 6:19-21 aloud to the class. Ask participants to discuss what this passage means to them. How do we store up treasures in heaven?

Work on a Personal Summary Picture
(25 Minutes)

Distribute sheets of paper to each participant. In order to help summarize what persons have learned about themselves so far halfway through the course and also to help those persons who learn best through images rather than words, tell participants that they will be drawing a summary picture of themselves, representing their spiritual gifts, their talents, and their resources. Realizing that not everyone has the talent of drawing, the picture need not be elaborate,

and can be as simple as a stick figure and very rough symbolic approximations of things. The person can be *doing* a talent; *have* a spiritual gift *inside*; and be *surrounded* by resources. So, for example, we might have a simple drawing of a person sitting at a piano, with an exclamation point drawn inside the person's head area, and with a cabin to one side of the person—with trees sur-  rounding the cabin and with smoke coming from the cabin's chimney.

The drawing would represent a talent of piano-playing; a spiritual gift of wisdom (the exclamation point in the head area); and a cabin in the woods that could be used by church groups for retreats.

Depending on available time, participants can include as many of their talents, spiritual gifts, and resources in their drawings as they are able.

Be sure to allow time for persons to share what they have drawn.

Whether you are doing a 60-minute session or a 120-minute session, you are now at the end of the session.

If this has been a 60-minute session, ask the participants to read the Individuality material in Chapter 5 for the next time.

If this has been a 120-minute session, tell the participants to read the Individuality material and the Dreams material in Chapters 5 and 6 before the next session.

Talents

I appeal to you therefore, brothers and sisters, by the mercies of God, to present your bodies as a living sacrifice, holy and acceptable to God, which is your spiritual worship. —Romans 12:1

The "T" in S.T.R.I.D.E. stands for our Talents—both God-given and acquired. Every person is born with natural talents, whether for athletics, music, arithmetic, mechanics, or something else altogether. Talents are those abilities that seem to "come naturally." See if you can identify the talents of the following people:

Michael Jordan _____

Barbra Streisand _____

Bill Gates _____

Maya Angelou_____

Sometimes we confuse talents with spiritual gifts. They can seem very similar, because both refer to an exceptional ability to do something. Natural abilities may mirror gifts, but there are some differences. Spiritual gifts are given to Christians, while every person (Christian or not) is born with natural talents. Talents are sometimes used to benefit others, but they can also be used for self-edification. Spiritual gifts are used to glorify God and to serve others.

One way to distinguish whether an ability is a talent or a spiritual gift is to consider the purpose and the results. Does the ability serve others and glorify God? Spiritual gifts will have a "yes" answer to both of these questions.

Acquired skills and expertise can be used to serve others and glorify God as well. Public speaking, facilitation skills, writing, and expertise in computers, graphic arts, or audio/video technology can all have a place serving within the Body of Christ.

Sometimes people use their natural talents or acquired skills in concert with their spiritual gifts. For example, Oleta Adams, a wonderful blues singer from Kansas City, has a tremendous musical talent. She was raised as a child in the church (her father is a pastor), but she didn't have a personal faith in Christ. As an adult she sang in bars and clubs. When she came into a personal relationship with Christ, God gave her the spiritual gift of Exhortation. She now uses her natural musical talent with her spiritual gift of Exhortation by singing songs that glorify God. Her message strengthens and encourages others to follow Christ.

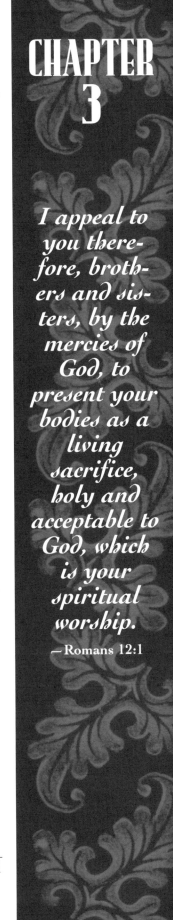

CHAPTER 3

I appeal to you therefore, brothers and sisters, by the mercies of God, to present your bodies as a living sacrifice, holy and acceptable to God, which is your spiritual worship.

—Romans 12:1

God can also *transform* our natural talents into spiritual gifts. For instance, God may elevate and amplify someone's natural leadership to the point of a spiritual gift when he or she enters into a believing relationship with Jesus Christ.

Some jobs or tasks cannot be completed without help from God. We have to be open to letting God work through us for great things to happen. In the Bible, when the Moabites and Ammonites came to make war against King Jehoshaphat and the Israelites in 2 Chronicles 20, Jehoshaphat called upon the Lord for help. The Lord answered him saying, "Do not fear or be dismayed at this great multitude; for the battle is not yours but God's." (2 Chronicles 20:15) The same is true for us today as we serve God. We need to "get out of the way" and let the Holy Spirit work through us. We are only the instruments.

When Yvonne first agreed to teach Spiritual Gifts Discovery, she based her decision on the fact that she had experience speaking in front of groups, and she had studied the material. She thought that she could handle it on the merit of her own abilities. The first two classes did not go well. Finally, one evening after class, she went home in tears. She prayed to God, "Maybe I'm in the wrong place again! I can't do this! I need your help. Next week, I'll show up, but you'll have to teach the class. If you don't want me doing this, I'll know."

Amazingly, the next week it was if the Holy Spirit DID teach the class. Yvonne's speaking ability was used, but the difference was that now she was willing to allow the Holy Spirit to work through her, instead of relying on her own abilities.

What are your natural talents or acquired skills that God could use for God's purposes?

We need to recognize that all abilities come from God. In that sense, they are gifts and can be dedicated to God's use. What makes *spiritual* gifts distinct is that God owns the results. God gets the credit, because what is accomplished is beyond our own abilities. In the Bible passage that opens this chapter, Paul instructs us to "present our bodies as a living sacrifice." That means our whole selves—our gifts, our talents, our dreams, our individual styles, and our resources, which we'll cover next.

Notes/Reflections on Talents:

Resources

You did not choose me but I chose you. And I appointed you to go and bear fruit, fruit that will last, so that the Father will give you whatever you ask him in my name.

—John 15:16

When we think of resources, most of us usually think of financial resources. These are certainly a part of our resource pool, but there is so much more. Our resources include our finances, our time, our material possessions, our contacts, our hobbies, and many other items. The question we ask in this chapter is, "How do we best utilize the resources God has give us to have an impact for God's purposes?"

There is an old saying that goes something like this: "I've never seen a hearse towing a U-Haul® trailer behind it." The meaning is pretty clear—you can't take it with you. However, this saying leaves out an important teaching of Christ—you can't take it with you, *but you can send it on ahead.* In Matthew 6:19-21, Christ says these words:

> *"Do not store up for yourselves treasures on earth, where moth and rust consume and where thieves break in and steal; but store up for yourselves treasures in heaven, where neither moth nor rust consumes and where thieves do not break in and steal. For where your treasure is, there your heart will be also.*

Christ instructed us here to invest in things that have eternal value. Only two things are eternal: God and people. How do we invest in these? By being good stewards of our resources.

Jesus used a great parable to explain the stewardship of our resources. It is often called the parable of the talents. (Talents were a type of currency in Jesus' time.)

> *"For it is as if a man, going on a journey, summoned his slaves and entrusted his property to them; to one he gave five talents, to another two, to another one, to each according to his ability. Then he went away. The one who had received the five talents went off at once and traded with them, and made five more talents. In the same way, the one who had the two talents made two more talents. But the one who had received the one talent went off and dug a hole in the ground and hid his master's money. After a long time the master of those slaves came and settled accounts with them. Then the one who had received the five talents came forward, bringing five more talents, saying, 'Master, you handed over to me five talents; see, I have made five more talents.' His master said to him, 'Well done, good and trustworthy slave; you have been trustworthy in a few things, I will put you in charge of many things; enter into the joy of your master.' And the one with the two talents also came forward, saying, 'Master, you*

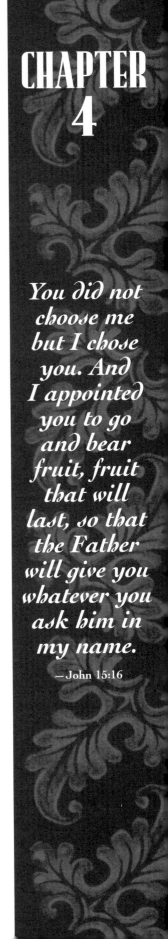

CHAPTER 4

You did not choose me but I chose you. And I appointed you to go and bear fruit, fruit that will last, so that the Father will give you whatever you ask him in my name.

—John 15:16

handed over to me two talents; see, I have made two more talents.' His master said to him, 'Well done, good and trustworthy slave; you have been trustworthy in a few things, I will put you in charge of many things; enter into the joy of your master.' Then the one who had received the one talent also came forward, saying, 'Master, I knew that you were a harsh man, reaping where you did not sow, and gathering where you did not scatter seed; so I was afraid, and I went and hid your talent in the ground. Here you have what is yours.' But his master replied, 'You wicked and lazy slave! You knew, did you, that I reap where I did not sow, and gather where I did not scatter? Then you ought to have invested my money with the bankers, and on my return I would have received what was my own with interest. So take the talent from him, and give it to the one with the ten talents. For to all those who have, more will be given, and they will have an abundance; but from those who have nothing, even what they have will be taken away. As for this worthless slave, throw him into the outer darkness, where there will be weeping and gnashing of teeth.'" (Matthew 25:14-30)

Have you ever heard the saying, "From those to whom much is given, much will be expected?" This is the message of this parable. We all receive much from God. All that we have is from God. What we have is not ours to keep for ourselves—or to hide in a hole in the ground—but is ours to use while we are here on earth. We are only stewards of all that we have. How can you put your resources to use for God?

Investing in things that are eternal also includes setting priorities based on our values, and then living by those priorities. The story of Mary and Martha is an example of this. Mary and Martha had different talents and resources, but where do you think the priority could have been for both? You may remember the story. Jesus was visiting their house. . .

Now as they went on their way, he entered a certain village, where a woman named Martha welcomed him into her home. She had a sister named Mary, who sat at the Lord's feet and listened to what he was saying. But Martha was distracted by her many tasks; so she came to him and asked, "Lord, do you not care that my sister has left me to do all the work by myself? Tell her then to help me." But the Lord answered her, "Martha, Martha, you are worried and distracted by many things; there is need of only one thing. Mary has chosen the better part, which will not be taken away from her." (Luke 10:38-42)

We can use our material resources in many ways to glorify God. One member of our church has a small farm with animals. She volunteers the use of her donkey and lamb for our Christmas pageant every year. Another member opens her home to members of the church for fellowship activities. Yet another member bakes fabulous bread for various events.

Our contacts (the people in our address books) are resources, too. Perhaps we can ask them to speak to our Sunday school class or other group. Maybe they can help with a project or be a resource for ideas or information.

What are your resources?

How can you use them to serve others and to glorify God?

Notes/Reflections on Resources:

SESSION 5
INDIVIDUALITY

OBJECTIVE FOR THIS SESSION:

To discover one's own individuality and the implications for the ways style can affect serving God in church and community.

Prepare by reading in advance the material in Chapter 5 in the workbook, and in Session 5 in the leader's guide. Read all Bible passages for yourself. Try all instructions given both in the workbook and the leader's guide.

Watch the CD-ROM video segment, "Chapter 5, Individuality." If you are using the overhead slides, either print the overheads for Session 5 for use on a projector or bring the disk for use with a computer and projector.

Materials Needed: pens or pencils; white board or newsprint with appropriate markers; Bibles; workbooks

Welcome and Pray *(5 minutes)*
Welcome participants back and open with prayer asking for God to bless the uniqueness of each individual present and to use that uniqueness in ways that serve others and glorify God.

Introduce the Concept of Individuality *(5 minutes)*
Since most participants will not have read Chapter 5, you will have to share the infor-

mation you have read from that chapter. Note: While our indivdual personalities and preferences help to make each one of us unique, no type is better or worse than any other. However, personality traits might make individuals better suited for particular ways of serving and less so for others. It is because of this that understanding our own individuality becomes so important and helpful. We will be more joyful and effective if we serve in ways that mesh better with our own unique personality, even though we might stretch ourselves to serve in ways that do not exactly match if the need arises.

Understanding Personality Type *(15 minutes)*
On the white board or newsprint, draw a horizontal line. Label the line, "Personality Type." Mark "Extrovert" at the left end, and "Introvert" at the right end.

Explain that one of the two important

For more reading about personality types described around energy, organizing and information needs, see:

Please Understand Me II: Temperment, Character, Intelligence, Peter Keirsey, Prometheus Nemesis Book Co, May 1998

Gifts Differing by Isabel Briggs-Myers, Consulting Psychologists Press, August 1980.

Groups and individuals can arrange to take the Myers Briggs Type Indicator through a certified trainer in your area. Briefer, less statistical testing tools can often be found on the internet.

---

components of Individuality that we will look at today is a broad description of personality type. Tell the class that the terms "introvert" and "extrovert" were first used by psychiatrist Carl Jung (1875-1961), and since then scholars and scientists have been exploring personality differences, examining how individuals take in the world and happenings around them, renew their energy and, through other type distinctions, how we process information, schedule our time and express our feelings.

Caution that popular use of the terms introvert and extrovert sometimes describes people by how shy or outgoing they appear. That can be misleading. We'll focus on looking at **how** individuals differ in the way they renew their energy. Where you find your energy and where you recharge may be much more helpful in discovering your best matches for service.

Psychologists like Carl Jung, Isabel Briggs-Myers and David Keirsey have written about the differences between introverts and extroverts and their energy sources. Members of the class may have taken the Myers-Briggs Type Indicator or the Keirsey Temperament Sorter. Ask members who have taken such assessments what they learned about themselves.

What are the differences between introverts and extroverts? How are we energized? Where do we find our energy? How are our batteries recharged? Are we drained from energy by being among people and then have to go off by ourselves for awhile to recover? Or are we energized by people but then go bonkers if we are stuck by ourselves for too long? That's the primary difference between introverts and extroverts. It's not so much shyness over against being outgoing; it's a matter of how one receives

and expends energy.

Ask participants to work individually on the questions on pages 36 to 37 in their workbook, dealing with energy focus. Allow about five minutes.

Check whether anyone is still unsure whether he/she is an extrovert or an introvert. If anyone is, ask that person's permission to allow the group to help in figuring out that person's energy focus from that person's responses on the questions.

Ask participants to mark where they would place themselves on the Extrovert-Introvert continuum on page 38 of their workbook.

Understanding Your Preferred Environment (15 minutes)

On the white board or newsprint, draw a horizontal line below the "Personality Type" horizontal line you have already drawn. Label the line, "PREFERRED ENVIRONMENT." Mark "Flexible" at the left end, and "Stable" at the right end.

Explain that the other important component of Individuality involves our preferred environment. Specifically, how do we feel about structure in our work? Do we want everything laid out and predictable? Or do we want to be independent as we do things? This is the realm of stability over against flexibility.

Ask participants to work individually on the questions on pages 38 to 39 in their workbook, dealing with preferred environment. Allow about five minutes.

Check whether anyone is still unsure whether he/she prefers stability or flexibility. If anyone is, ask that person's permission to allow the group to help in figuring out that person's preferred environment from that person's responses on the questions.

Ask participants to mark where they would place themselves on the Flexible-Stable continuum on page 40 of their workbook.

Put the Components Together *(20 minutes)*
You have already drawn two axes on the white board or newsprint. Ask participants to come up to the chart and write their initials roughly where their location would be on each axis. This will help them to see that there are varying degrees within each component. Combining the choices from the Personality Type axis and the Preferred Environment axis, you have four possible combinations: extroverts who prefer stability, extroverts who prefer flexibility, introverts who prefer stability and introverts who prefer flexibility. Because of differing degrees in each area, even persons who share the same combination will yet be unique individuals. The closer one is towards the center of each axis, the more likely one may be able to take on the characteristics of another type as need arises.

Ask persons who share a personality/environment combination to form small groups together. If a particular one of the four groups has too many participants in it, you might want to split it into yet smaller groups. One member groups are okay for this activity. The assignment is to read over and discuss as a group the material found on pages 40 to 42 in the workbook pertaining to their particular combination. Small groups should discuss (1) whether the descriptions fit their experience; (2) whether they feel drawn to the church ministries suggested for that combination; and (3) what they think of the word of caution given for that combination.

Optional Closing
Prayerfully listen to the music selection "The Lord's Prayer/Collect for Purity" on the Leader CD. (The CD will play in regular CD players.) These two prayers have been used in the church since the 8th or 9th centuries. Listen to the power and relevance they offer today.

Collect for Purity
Almighty God, unto whom all hearts are
   open,
all desires are known, and from whom no
secrets are hid: Cleanse the thoughts of our
hearts by the inspiration of thy Holy Spirit,
   that
we may perfectly love thee, and worthily
   magnify
thy holy Name; through Christ our Lord.
   Amen.

If you are doing only a 60-minute session, end the session by praying for God to watch over each participant as they ponder the needs of the world around them. For next time, read Chapter 6, Dreams.
If you are doing a 120-minute session, go on to Session 6 in this leader's guide now.

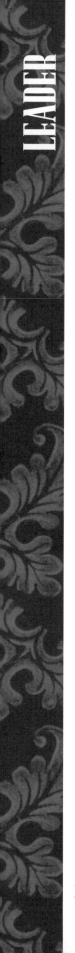

Individuality

There is one body and one Spirit, just as you were called to the one hope of your calling, one Lord, one faith, one baptism, one God and Father of all, who is above all and through all and in all. But each of us was given grace according to the measure of Christ's gift.

—Ephesians 4:4-7

Just as, by God's design, no two snowflakes are exactly alike, God created people to be unique individuals. No one in all of God's creation is exactly like you. That is amazing even to think about. You are a genuine, one-copy original, with a style all your own.

Considering our individuality is important as we consider the ways in which we will serve God. Our style affects the way we think, expend and receive our energy, organize our work, and interact with other people. Many instruments are available today to help people determine their style or personality type. Perhaps you have taken one through your employer, community group, or church.

For simplicity's sake, we shall focus on two key components of individuality that most directly impact service: (1) personality type and (2) preferred environment. In our discussion of personality, we'll talk about extroverts and introverts. When we shift to preferred environment, we'll focus on whether you prefer a flexible or stable environment.

Can we determine a person's style just by watching them? Not necessarily. For instance, Carmen speaks quite well in front of groups and seems to make small talk with ease. She introduces herself to new people and makes them feel welcome to the group. She always has a smile on her face and is usually the first one to tell a joke. What do you think: extrovert or introvert? Actually, Carmen is an extreme introvert, but her career as a business owner requires her to operate outside of her instinctive style. She took a course in public speaking and human relations to help her get out of her "comfort zone." Now she does those things with seeming effortlessness, but they are still not "comfortable" to her. They are not natural actions, but learned behaviors.

As you go through this chapter, try to focus on what is "natural" for you—what is instinctive—not what you have learned to do or what is required of you in your career, family, or other environment.

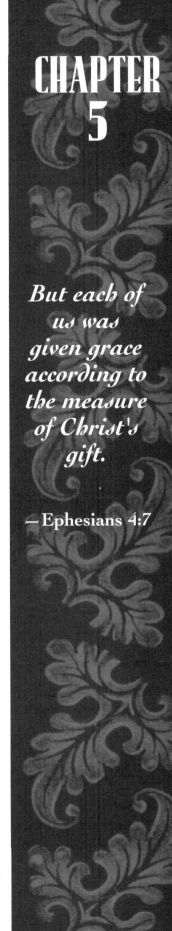

CHAPTER 5

But each of us was given grace according to the measure of Christ's gift.

—**Ephesians 4:7**

Personality Type

Depending on the way you are "wired," you are either considered an *introvert* or an *extrovert*. Since 1921, when psychiatrist Carl Jung (1875-1961) wrote *Psychological Types*, scholars and scientists have been exploring personality differences. Jung wrote about the now famous types, "introverts" and "extroverts" examining how individuals take in the world, renew their energy and, through other type distinctions, how we process information, schedule our time and express our feelings. People sometimes misunderstand the dynamics of these words, believing that extroverts are boisterous, gregarious, outgoing individuals, while introverts are quiet, reserved, and humble. While this may be the case in some instances, these views are stereotypes. The terms *introvert* and *extrovert* have more to do with the ways in which we receive and expend energy—or our energy focus—than how verbal we may or may not be.

Another way to look at personality types, building on this work, can be found in David Keirsey's writing. He suggests that some people gain energy, like being powered by batteries, from other people. Long periods of quiet and individual work are exhausting for them. Others draw energy from solitary activities, working alone on a project that captures their passion whether it is simple or difficult. These individuals because exhausted in large groups or from extended contact with others. Of course, these examples represent extremes. Most people find themselves somewhere between the two extremes. Where they find themselves may also very well depend upon their circumstances.

Why is it important to understand your personality type when you are considering where to serve? Well, let's think about that for minute. . . . If you prefer to interact with a lot of people, and you volunteer to serve in an area where you are performing behind-the-scenes functions with little opportunity to be with other people, how might that make you feel? Restless? Bored? Closed off? On the other hand, if you like to work quietly to accomplish goals, interacting with people on occasion, how would you feel if the position in which you serve puts you in a large group of people with little time for working on projects and gives you no quiet time to yourself? Frustrated? Uncomfortable?

You may immediately know whether your type is more extroverted or introverted. Just in case you don't, here are a few questions that may help you determine your personality type.

Try to answer using the word that best describes what you prefer, not what your current work, church, or home circumstances dictate. Circle the word or phrase that best matches how you would complete each statement, and make notes or comments in the space allowed. A few questions are included after each statement for you to think about as you consider a potential ministry position.

I usually: *enjoy center stage* <u>or</u> *shun the limelight.*

> Think about this in a ministry setting. If the position requires you to be the focus of attention often, will it energize you or will it make you uncomfortable?

People who meet me would describe me as: *easy to get to know* or *quiet and reserved*.

As you consider a ministry position, will you be asked to meet new people often? How would you like that? Or will you develop relationships with a more stable group of people? Which is more to your liking?

I develop ideas through: *discussion* or *internal thought*.

Will you be required to share your thoughts and feelings in a group setting? Or will you be asked to develop ideas and then present them? Which do you prefer?

When my work is interrupted, I: *welcome the diversion* or *get impatient with the distraction*.

As you think about a particular ministry position, will there be many interruptions as you go about the task? Do you enjoy that? Or will that be a bother to you?

I work best: *in a group* or *independently*.

Some people really enjoy working with a group, while others enjoy more solitary pursuits. Which is your preference? When you consider stepping into a ministry position, consider whether it is a good fit with this preference.

I prefer to communicate with people via: *telephone* or *e-mail*.

Some ministry positions have a lot of personal communication with others, while some positions involve a lot of e-mail communication in between a small amount of personal contact. Which is more your style?

When my "batteries" need recharging, I: *go out with friends* or *spend some quiet time alone*.

This question is important as you consider a place of service. Will the position allow you to get your batteries recharged according to your preference? Make sure the position you serve in is not one that only "drains your batteries" without permitting you time and opportunity for "recharging."

How did you answer these questions? If you circled the first choice in the two statements, you are more likely to be an extrovert. If more of the second answers fit, you are more likely to be an introvert. Still can't decide? In meetings, do you tend to "think out loud?" Or do you usually consider your thoughts and ideas carefully before sharing them? Think about what you do when you are tired or stressed out. Do you get together with friends to "forget about it" or "get recharged?" Or are you more likely to need time alone to just "chill?" Do you find it easy to talk to just about anyone you meet? Or is it easier for you to talk to people you have known for a while? Consider your instinctive responses, not what you have learned to do.

Remember that most of us fit somewhere in between the two extremes, and in fact operate all along the continuum, moving back and forth during our day. Usually, though, we are more comfortable and would prefer to operate in one place most of the time. When we serve in an area that is opposite of our preference, we *can* do it, but after a while, doing so will drain us of our energy, instead of making us feel energized.

Take a look at the continuum below and think about where you fit. Make a mark there:

|_____|_____|

Extrovert   Middle   Introvert
energized   energized
through   through
interaction   reflection

Finding yourself near the middle of the continuum may simply mean that situations in which you find yourself will dictate your preferred response.

Remember: Extroverts also accomplish tasks and introverts also love people. The purpose of this exercise is to determine which of the two scenarios recharge your batteries and revive your spirit. When it comes to serving God in the church or out in the community, you will want to find yourself in a place of service where you are energized rather than where you are constantly drained of energy.

Preferred Environment

The term *environment* describes how you prefer to work in any setting. This means what you do in the context of your job, at home, in the church, or anyplace where you do anything. In order to accomplish the task at hand, people tend to prefer either a *stable* environment or a *flexible* one.

Generally speaking, a person who prefers a stable environment likes to work with the realm of deadlines, structure, accountability, and systems. He or she will find systems freeing and comfortable, because then they know exactly what to expect and what is expected of them. Individuals who prefer a flexible environment find structure, deadlines, and systems to be confining. The "flexible" person prefers to focus on the end product, leaving the details of how to get there subject to change and interpretation.

Let's talk about why this might be important. If you prefer flexibility in your environment, and you serve in an area that requires you to follow specific steps to accomplish your goals with no room for "interpretation," how would you feel? Stifled? Bored? Or if you prefer a stable environment, and you serve in an area where things are always changing, where you never do the same thing twice or the same thing twice the same way, how would that make you feel? Uncomfortable? Insecure?

Once again, you may be able to identify immediately your own preferred environment. Just in case you can't, the following exercise is designed to help you make a determination about where you might fit on the continuum. Keep in mind, as you did with the previous exercise, to answer the questions based upon your own preference, not on the situations in which you currently find yourself at work, at home, in your community, or at church, Make any notes or comments in the space provided.

When I'm working on a project, I like to: *adapt as I go* <u>or</u> *plan ahead*.

When you are considering a place of service, think about the structure that may be required. If you "plan your work and then work your plan," but the position requires a great deal of flexibility and many last minute changes, will you feel stressed?

I tend to work with: *spurts of energy at the last minute* or *regular, steady effort*.

If you work in bursts of energy, will the position allow you that freedom, or will it require meeting deadlines all along the way? On the other hand, if you like regular, steady effort, will there be enough structure and focus to keep you happy?

When I plan my activities, the plans are: *"penciled in"* or *final*.

Do you like to "keep your options open" or do you prefer to make decisions and move on? Think about how you plan your vacation. Do you make a general plan for activities that is open to change, or do you make reservations for every activity? Consider whether the ministry position you are considering will be a good "fit" for you in this regard.

I like: *spontaneity* or *predictability*.

Do you feel more comfortable when you know what to expect? Or do you get bored with routine? Think about how this might apply to a ministry setting. If the position is the same

every day, will you be relaxed and confident, or will you be bored silly?

I tend to: *have several projects going on at once* or *finish one thing before going on to the next*.

Think about your typical "to do" list. Do you check everything off, or do you often get most things completed and leave others for another day? Will the position require multi-tasking, or will it require a step-by-step process, one project at a time? Which is more to your liking?

I prefer decisions that are: *open to discussion* or *provide closure*.

When you make decisions, or hear a decision that someone else has made, think about your response. When you make a decision do you consider it final, or do you still feel open to input from others and the possibility of changing your mind? If someone else makes the decision, do you get annoyed if they later change their decision, or do you admire their flexibility? How might this apply in a ministry setting?

I usually dress for: *comfort* or *appearance*.

Think about your "style." Do you like to dress casually, more for comfort and convenience than for fashion? Or do you prefer to look neat and "finished." Consider this in broader terms than dress. Are you more of a serious person, or a more light-hearted person? Do you like to be in control, or do you like to "wait and see?" Will the ministry position be a good fit in this regard?

How did you answer the questions. Do you prefer a stable or a more flexible environment? If you were more likely to choose the first response in each pair, you are more likely to prefer a flexible enviornment. If the second responses seem to fit more often, you may find a stable environment more appealing. Can't decide? Think about a project you have worked on? Did you form a general plan, but then adapt and change course when you thought it was appropriate? Or did you plan everything in detail and then follow that plan? Do you mix work and play? Or do you follow the mantra, *work before play*? Do you get excited when you start a project? Or do you get more pleasure out of finishing a project? Take a look at the continuum and think about where you fit. Place a mark there:

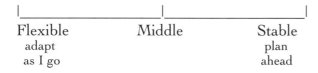

Flexible   Middle   Stable
adapt   plan
as I go   ahead

Hopefully, answering these questions has aided you in determining your preferred environment. In some instances, both word choices might fit you. However, you will still likely have a preference for one over the other, slight though it may be. For example, the flexible person might love multiple options when working on a project, but still long for closure at some point. If you do not fall neatly into one category or the other, take heart. Try to give thought to the very

best environment you can imagine and prepare yourself to articulate your needs for a service setting. You will find less frustration when you can clearly choose a place to serve God that is in harmony with the unique way in which God has created you.

Putting It All Together

On the space below, write out the combination of energy focus and preferred environment that best describes you (extrovert/stable; extrovert/flexible; introvert/stable; introvert/flexible):

I am

_____ .

Now it's time to take the next step and consider what these style combinations mean when it comes to serving God. Remember at the start of this chapter when you read about the implications of style? *Our individuality affects the way we think, receive and expend our energy, organize our work, and interact with other people.* Let's connect these concepts to serving God in the church and community for each of the four style combinations. While we are suggesting some areas where each of these types might work or serve, remember that many other things need to be considered: your spiritual gifts, what you are passionate about, your talents and acquired skills, and so forth. So don't be discouraged if the suggestions are not right for you. As we said in the beginning, *you are unique!*

Extrovert/Stable

If you are an extrovert/stable individual, then you may be energized by interaction with people, but you will likely prefer to interact with people in predetermined settings and at scheduled times. You value effectiveness and efficiency, tend to be practical, yet are outgoing and warm.

Communication with this type of person should be personal, goals need to be specific, and any service must be relevant to the needs of another.

Preferred careers for those with this type combination may be counselors, social workers, child-care providers, small business owners, health care workers, and receptionists. In the church—based solely upon style—you may be drawn to people-oriented service opportunities such as Stephen's Ministry, small group leadership, greeter, usher, hospitality provider, recognition team member, intercessory prayer, nursery or pre-school, or a mission ministry with direct but predictable people contact.

A word of caution: this type tends to over-commit to work and over-invest emotionally.

Extrovert/Flexible

If you are an extrovert/flexible individual, you are energized by people-interaction. You enjoy more spontaneity and less structure, more fun and less practicality. You value creativity, exude enthusiasm, welcome change, and have the capacity to be engaging and inspirational. Communication with this type of person should be direct and frequent, goals need to be "big picture," and the best service opportunity will capitalize on the ability to market and promote the ministry.

Preferred careers for the extrovert/flexible person might be marketing personnel, politicians, actors, consultants, teachers, and sales agents. Within the church, this type of person might be well-suited for a ministry opportunity involving team-building, event planning, youth group leading, teaching

Bible classes and workshops, drama team directing, or marketing new programs.

A work of caution: this type may lose sight of important details or have trouble keeping enough focus to accomplish the goal.

Introvert/Stable

If you are an introvert/stable individual, you tend to be quiet, reflective, and practical. You learn through research and observation. You value consistency and preservation. In your opinion, systems, policies, and procedures were designed to be followed to the letter. Communication with this type of person should be direct and detailed, goals need to be practical, and service in the church must be organized and reliable.

Preferred careers might include accountants, school principals, carpenters, clerical supervisors, clergy, military officers, and technicians in various fields. If you are this type of person, every ministry area will desire you to help organize the necessary details and weigh all the options. You might be drawn to serve in the financial or facilities ministries of the church, help with the office work including collating bulletins or mailings, edit publications, or help with audio-visual and computer technology ministries.

A word of caution: this type can exhibit nit-picking tendencies, become bogged down with details, or lose sight of the "big picture."

Introvert/Flexible

If you are an introvert/flexible individual, you tend to be direct, visionary, focused, confident, and competitive. You value results, big dreams, thorough research, and independent thinking.

Communication with this type of person should be direct and concise, goals should be visionary, and a service position in the church must include versatility, general guidelines, and reasonable authority.

If you are this type of person, you may be drawn to a career as a lawyer, architect, senior pastor, manager or executive, engineer, journalist, or physician. In the church, you might consider leading a team or committee, organizing an event or campaign, teaching Sunday school, leading a mission trip, or serving as a group facilitator.

A word of caution: this type may be perceived as pushy, controlling, or arrogant, and would do well to remember that the thoughts, ideas, and contributions of others are valuable and necessary.

Conclusion

Every ministry area and team within the church benefits from having each of the four combinations represented. A ministry or program stands a better chance of succeeding with each of these in balance. Goals will be set and met, people inspired and challenged, details organized efficiently, and everyone's efforts encouraged and celebrated. God will be glorified!

When it comes to dealing with people, they will not always fit neatly on a grid or continuum. We have to let go of linear thinking and remember that human beings are much more complex and diverse. They cannot be pigeon-holed into a category. Yet knowing our individual style—and the styles of those with whom we interact—can provide important clues to help us communicate more effectively, avoid conflict, articulate our service environment needs, and serve with less frustration and more joy. That is precisely what God wants for us. . . a place to serve and glorify God where we can be our best selves, fulfilling God's perfect design!

Notes/Reflections on Individuality:

SESSION 6
DREAMS

If you are doing four 120-minute sessions, you will pick up here immediately following the end of Session 5. You will probably wish to take a 5-minute break before starting in on the material contained here in Session 6.

If you are doing eight 60-minute sessions, Session 6 is a separate, stand-alone session.

OBJECTIVE FOR THIS SESSION:

To begin the work of discovering the particular dream or passion God has placed in each person's heart.

Prepare by reading in advance the material in Chapter 6 in the workbook, and in Session 6 in the leader's guide. Read all Bible passages for yourself. Try all instructions given both in the workbook and the leader's guide.

Note that you will have to prepare according to one of two plans for the segment, "Be Touched by a Dream." In *Plan A* you will be projecting the color slides to the group. This will require you to use the leader's CD-ROM with a lap-top computer, LCD projector, and screen to show the slide show or you may print the slide show on overhead transparency slides and project with an overhead projector. *Plan B* will require you to use the CD-ROM to *print out* a set of the pictures from the slide show. You will then need to post those pictures at eye level around the room or, preferably, a nearby area in advance.

Watch the CD-ROM video segment, "Chapter 6, Dreams." If you are using the overhead slides, either print the overheads for Session 6 for use on a projector or bring the disk for use with a computer and projector.

Materials Needed: blank paper; pens or pencils; white board or newsprint with appropriate markers; Bibles; workbooks; for *Plan A:* the CD-ROM, a lap top computer, an LCD projector and a projection screen or transparencies and an overhead projector; or for *Plan B:* a set of pictures from the CD-ROM, printed out and posted in advance.

If You Are Starting a 60-Minute Session *(5 minutes)*

Welcome participants back and open with prayer thanking God for spiritual gifts, talents, resources, individual styles, and dreams that assist in finding the best ways to serve God.

Introduce the Concept of Dreams and Passions *(10 minutes)*

Since most participants will not have read Chapter 6, you will have to share the information you have read from that chapter. Note especially that dreams and passions are difficult for most people to pin down. Although what we are really talking about here has to do with the calling or vocation God is giving to us, most of us have difficulty clearly perceiving it.

Also note that when we speak of *dreams* here, we are not necessarily referring to the dreams we have when we sleep. To be sure, at times God's Holy Spirit may show us things through our dreams; however, we are using the word *dreams* here differently—to mean the dreams God places in our hearts to help us understand the specific ways in which God wants us to serve other persons to God's glory. And so we might have a *dream* that we tutor underprivileged children in our neighborhood, or a *dream* that we serve as first responders in case of disasters somewhere in our state, or a *dream* that we polish the brassware throughout the chancel area so that it gleams every Sunday for the glory of God.

God will give us passion for that which God calls us to do. But sometimes we will have to learn about that passion through trial and error. While most of us have a notion of some things we *know* we *don't* want to do, we may have to try out some things before we find the one or two things that we discover we strongly have an urge to do.

Be Touched by a Dream—Plan A
(45 minutes)

Ask participants to turn to Session Six to the Touched by a Dream form on page 48. (You can also copy the page from this book.) Tell the participants that you will be showing them 32 pictures. As they watch the pictures, they are to keep track of which ones "grab" them or engage them. They are not to *think* about the pictures or *analyze* them; rather they are to *feel* about them. Participants should put a check or "x" beside the number of each picture that engages them. They might also write a few words about what touched them. Show the pictures without comment, changing pictures every fifteen seconds. (The slide show will take about ten minutes.)

After showing the slides or viewing the pictures, read the class the descriptions of each of the 32 pictures. Ask participants to jot down descriptions by the pictures that had particularly moved them. Allow persons individual time to look over their lists. Ask them to look over the words jotted down and the descriptions you read. Do they see any patterns in the photos they chose? If patterns do show up, those patterns might indicate a dream or a passion. For example, if the word *hunger* shows up several time on someone's sheet of paper because he or she was moved by several pictures of people suffering from hunger, perhaps that individual has been given a dream—a passion—of working in some way to combat hunger. Or maybe another individual notes that she or he has mentioned several different kinds of carpentry tools that showed up in pictures. That might mean that this person has a passion that could be fulfilled by working with a volunteer mission team working on a construction project or with a Habitat for Humanity housing project.

Next, divide the participants into small groups of three persons. Each person will have five minutes to share her or his insights into what her or his dreams and passions might be. If time allows within the five minutes, she or he may invite feedback from the other two members of the small group; however, the full five minutes is to be focused on that individual's dreams and passions. You as leader will need to keep strict track of time in order to tell participants when it is time to move to the second and the third small group member.

Be Touched by a Dream— Plan B

(45 minutes)

Plan B is the same as Plan A, except that instead of viewing the CD-ROM based slide show, participants will view posted pictures with the same set of instructions. Allow ten minutes for viewing the pictures.

Proceed with the same directions as for Plan A.

Note to Leaders: The slides show a variety of mission and ministry opportunities, but some programs important to your church or region may not be represented. It is easy to add new digital photos to the slide show by inserting new slide pages and adding your own pictures.

Whether you are doing a 60-minute session or a 120-minute session, you are now at the end of the session.

Whether this has been a 60-minute or a 120-minute session, tell the participants that their assignment for next time is to read Chapter 7 in the workbook. Ask them to consider how the insights they gain from working through Chapter 6 mesh with the insights they have gained from this session.

Close with prayer asking God to provide clarity to the dreams and calling of these people.

Be Touched by a Dream

Show the slides or printouts to the students with little information or explanation so that they can record their emotional response to the pictures. After the participants have seen the slides and checked the pictures that engaged them, read the class the descriptions below. The description reminds the viewer of the images in the photo and then, in italics, the possibilities of what may have appealed including the type of individual helped (a child), a particular issue (health care) or a role of service (administrator, teacher). The descriptions do not cover all the concepts in each picture – and some pictures can be interpreted several ways so expect some discussion.

1. Afghan refugees — *Refugees, families*
2. Ambulance in Liberia — *Health care, fundraising, world mission*
3. Asian women in worship service — *Worship arts*
4. Rolling out carpet at Conference — *Set up, administration*
5. Men looking through bars, Cuba — *Oppressed, civil rights*
6. Deaf Choir worship performance — *Worship arts, music, disabilities*
7. Handbell performance — *Worship arts, music*
8. At the computer — *Technical skills, administration*
9. Rebuilding project after hurricane — *Building, disaster relief*
10. Men with lost limbs and crutches — *Health care, landmine relief*
11. African schoolroom — *Children, teaching*

12. Protestor with sign*	*Civil issues, protest, organization*
13. Father and child	*Families, Children*
14. Woman on the phone	*Organizing, administration*
15. Children's program, theatre set	*Children, Christian education, drama*
16. Food bank shelves	*People in need, hunger, organization*
17. Children on newly built bridge	*Children, building*
18. Sound/video technician	*Technical skills, media*
19. Building ground breaking	*Building, housing needs*
20. Native American children	*Children, recreation, teaching*
21. Clothes bank	*People in need, organization*
22. Teen and infant in clinic	*Children, health care*
23. Young girl	*Children*
24. Volunteer, tolerance rally*	*Civil issues, tolerance/diversity*
25. Man reading in doorway	*Education, world mission*
26. 911 Memorial Fence	*People grieving, disaster relief*
27. Father, girls on bike going to school	*Children, families, education*
28. Church damaged by tornado	*Disaster relief*
29. Food bank	*People in need, hunger, organization*
30. Shoe Collection Project	*People in need, organization*
31. Glasses for the Masses Project	*People in need, health care, organization*
32. Teen in clinic for eye test	*Teens, health care*

*To the Leader: Note that the viewer may agree or diasgree with the position expressed in the slide, but does it inspire the desire to speak out as a person of faith either for or against important issues?

Dreams

Hope deferred makes the heart sick, but a desire fulfilled is a tree of life.

—Proverbs 13:12

In his book, *The Call*, Os Guinness writes, "The truth is not that God is finding us a place for our gifts but that God has created us and our gifts for a place of His choosing."[1] Wayne Cordeiro, pastor of New Hope Christian Fellowship in Hawaii, put it his way, "If getting you to heaven were God's only reason for saving you, then the moment you would have received Christ as your Lord and Savior, God would have killed you! That's right. Now that you are saved, His job would be complete…But that wasn't the only reason He saved you. Instead of taking you immediately home, He placed a message in your heart. . . now there's a purpose to your life. There's a plan He has for you! Soon, your life and mine will be over, but until He takes you home, we have a message to deliver!"[2]

God cares about every need that exists on earth. God does not want anyone to be hurting, or sick, or alone, or lost. God counts on us to be God's hands and voice in this broken world; but God knows that we, as individuals, can't possibly care about every need. For that reason, much like a parent dividing household chores among children, God places a dream (a desire, a passion, a calling) in each of our hearts.

In his book, *Doing Church as a Team*, Wayne Cordeiro writes, "In every person's heart is a dream of what he or she can become for the Lord; a dream that sees them making a difference in the world, in their families, in their churches."[3] Unlike household chores, though, God makes us passionate about the calling God has for us. Because we are passionate about it, we are happy and successful when we are serving in that area. If each of us understands the dream that God has given us, and fulfills that calling, the Body of Christ can meet every need, heal every hurt, and save every lost lamb.

Where is it that you would like to make a difference? For a few people, this may seem simple. Most people struggle with it, however. We have heard many people say things like, "I'm not really passionate about anything!" One thing is for sure: Most of us have a clear understanding of

[1] Os Guinness, The Call: Finding and Fulfilling the Central Purpose of Your Life, (Nashville, TN: W Publishing Group, 1998), page 47.
[2] Wayne Cordiero, Doing Church as a Team, (Ventura, CA:Gospel Light Publications, December 2000, revised), page 26.
[3] Wayne Cordiero, Doing Church as a Team, (Ventura, CA:Gospel Light Publications, December 2000, revised), page 111.

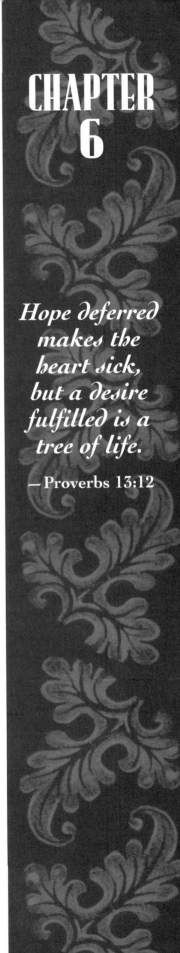

CHAPTER 6

Hope deferred makes the heart sick, but a desire fulfilled is a tree of life.

—Proverbs 13:12

what we *don't* want to do! Since we will not feel fulfilled until we're serving in an area about which we are passionate, we have a real need to discover our dreams. Guinness writes, "In many cases, a clear sense of calling comes only through a time of searching, including trial and error."[4] If you have never been exposed to the area in which God wants you to serve, you will probably not recognize it until you do try it out.

"Trial and error" can be intimidating. It means taking risks and just trying something! When you think about it, what makes it worthwhile to take such risks? Such risks are worthwhile because they make us utterly dependent upon God, not on ourselves. When we try serving in a new area, we are blazing a new trail in our life. Having the faith to risk stepping out of our comfort zone stretches us, and makes the journey more real.

The Body of Christ should be an environment where we are free to take such risks—free to fail with a group of supporters to pick us up, brush us off, and put us back in the saddle again (or maybe in a different saddle!).

Sometimes we are afraid because we are being called into an area that seems beyond our capabilities or experience. Thankfully, it's not our own capabilities or experience on which we have to rely, but on the power of the Holy Spirit. We look through a peep-

If I'm not free to fail, I'm not free to take risks, and everything in life that's worth doing involves a willingness to take a risk and involves a risk of failure. . . . I have to try, but I do not have to succeed. Following Christ has nothing to do with success as the world sees success.[6]
—Madeleine L'Engle

hole, while God encourages us to open the door and see the whole panorama.

In his book, *What You Do Best in the Body of Christ*, Bruce Bugbee lists three types of dreams that seem to pop up again and again: dreams of making a difference for individual persons or groups of people; dreams of making a difference in connection with some worthwhile cause; and dreams of making a difference through some role or function. For example, some persons may dream of helping specific groups of people, such as elderly persons, or youth, or children who have suffered abuse. Others may dream of conquering AIDS, or hunger, or homelessness. Still others may dream of making a difference through mentoring, or promoting stewardship, or using skills or specific gifts. Don't limit your dreams to these categories, though; they may fall outside of them.[5]

Frank has always been nuts about gadgets. If it has buttons, switches, lights, or wires, he loves it! He volunteered to help out by handling the audio equipment during Saturday night worship. A year later, he was on staff part-time, handling all of the audio needs of the Church of the Resurrection. This work allows him to serve the Lord while doing something about which he's passionate.

Discovering your dream and then actually fulfilling it can change your life. Have you ever known someone who believed that

---

[4]Os Guinness, The Call: Finding and Fulfilling the central Purpose of Your Life, (Nashville, TN: W Publishing Group, 1998) page 52.
[5]Bruce Bugbee, What You Do Best in the Body of Christ, (Nashville, TN: Zondervan Publishing, 1995), pages 35-36.
[6]Madeleine L'Engle, quoted by Al Janssen, Choices for Graduates (Grand Rapids, MI:Baker Book House, 1988), page 26.

serving God was supposed to be drudgery? A cross to be carried? We do not believe that is God's intention. God wants God's children to be filled with joy. Serving in an area about which you are passionate is a blessing. It provides a compass, giving you direction about where to serve; motivation and energy, helping you avoid burnout; joy and fulfillment, reflecting your dreams that are becoming reality.

but those who wait for the LORD shall renew their strength, they shall mount up with wings like eagles, they shall run and not be weary, they shall walk and not faint.

—Isaiah 40:31

Let's take time now to answer a few questions that may point you in the direction of your dreams.

What excites you most about the world?

What angers you most about the world?

What would you do if you had time and money to do anything?

What do you enjoy doing so much that time seems to fly when you're doing it?

About what do your friends and family think you are passionate? The observations of others can be very telling.

For what are you most grateful today? For what are you least grateful? If you were to ask yourself these questions everyday, what pattern would you see?

What makes life worthwhile is having a big enough objective, something which catches our imagination and lays hold of our allegiance, and this the Christian has, in a way that no other man has. For what higher, more exalted, and more compelling goal can there be than to know God?[7]

—J. I. Packer

When have you felt most alive? What are the times of your life you would most like to repeat?

If you could do anything with no chance of failure, what would you do?

Is there something that you love to do so much that you cannot imagine yourself not doing it?

If you had only one year to live, what would you do?

Look for patterns in your answers. Are there issues or topics that keep coming up?

---

[7] J.I. Packer, *Knowing God* (Downers Grove, IL: InterVaristy Press, 1973), page 30.

Don't forget to ask others what they think. Others can often see passions in you that you don't recognize. Sometimes we're too close to circumstances to see patterns. As the old saying goes, "You can't see the forest for the trees."

Try using the process of elimination to discover where you dream. Sometimes it's easier to decide what you don't want to do, so use that as a place to start. For instance, Yvonne knows that she does not really enjoy working with elementary age children, so she eliminated that age group from her choices. She isn't particularly passionate about ministering to homeless people, either. She is compassionate toward them, but not *passionate*. In the end, by eliminating some groups or activities, she was able to focus on what she did want to do, and to which group she wanted to minister—adults seeking to find how God had designed them for ministry.

With what particular age group of people do you enjoy being? With which particular age group would you prefer not to work?

With what groups of people would you like to work (such as persons who are homeless, older adults, people going through divorces)? With which specific groups of people do you not feel drawn to work?

What activities do you really enjoy and would like to incorporate into ministry (such as gardening, music, sports, and so forth)?

Look over your top three spiritual gifts. Is there one that you would enjoy using regardless of the situation? Is there a skill or talent that you want to put to use somewhere, but don't have a specific ministry area in mind?

Is there a need somewhere that you have noticed and feel drawn to seeing addressed?

Have you been involved in a ministry in the past that you really enjoyed and in which you would like to be involved again? Is there one in which you were not so effective or fulfilled, and so you would not want to repeat? What made them good or not so good for you?

Finding your dream is more of a journey than an event. It often requires trying a few things out to see if you like them. It should be a prayerful process. Ask for God's guidance. It can take a while. But once you discover your dreams, you cannot help but work to see them realized. They are like an emotional magnet drawing you in.

> *If I say, "I will not mention him, or speak any more in his name," then within me there is something like a burning fire shut up in my bones; I am weary with holding it in, and I cannot.*
> —Jeremiah 20:9

This calls for a word of caution: Because recognizing our dreams involves our feelings and emotions, we need to be sure our dreams are in harmony with God's will. Our dreams and goals should never contradict God's word in the Bible.

Another thing to note regarding dreams: We have been asked many times, "Well, if this is God's dream for my life, should I quit my job and do this full time?" We have seen that happen. But most of the time, a person's work supports or subsidizes the dream, not replaces it.

Based on what I know now, my dream is

_____.

Don't get discouraged if you're not sure what your dream is yet. Remember that this is difficult for many people to identify. Sometimes you just have to try something (or a few things). Sometimes it's a matter of testing the waters by serving in a ministry area that seems interesting or attractive to you. Once you get involved, you might find something more specific within that ministry really speaking to your heart. Often we start

with a general idea of what we want to do and, as we serve, our focus narrows and becomes much clearer.

It's important that you don't get stuck here. Keep hiking down the trail. Trust God to reveal God's dream for you in God's own time.

Notes/Reflections on Dreams:

Touched by a Dream

1. _____

2. _____

3. _____

4. _____

5. _____

6. _____

7. _____

8. _____

9. _____

10. _____

11. _____

12. _____

13. _____

14. _____

15. _____

16. _____

17. _____

18. _____

19. _____

20. _____

21. _____

22. _____

23. _____

24. _____

25. _____

26. _____

27. _____

28. _____

29. _____

30. _____

31. _____

32. _____

SESSION 7
EXPERIENCES

OBJECTIVE FOR THIS SESSION:

To consider how God can use our past experiences for God's purposes.

Prepare by reading in advance the material in Chapter 7 in the workbook, and in Session 7 in the leader's guide. Read all Bible passages for yourself. Try all instructions given both in the workbook and the leader's guide.

Make sure there is plenty of table work space for the "Learn from Experiences" activity.

Watch the CD-ROM video segment, "Chapter 7, Experiences." If you are using the overhead slides, either print the overheads for Session 7 for use on a projector or bring the disk for use with a computer and projector.

Materials Needed: blank paper; pens or pencils; colorful construction paper; small blank stickers, approximately 1" x ¾" (available at any office supply store or store that sells school supplies) for each participant; Bibles; workbooks.

Welcome and Pray (*5 minutes*)

Welcome participants back and open with prayer praising God as the God of the past as well as of the present and the future.

Review Dreams and Passions (*10 minutes*)

Ask participants to share briefly about further insights they have had since the last meeting about their dreams and passions, especially as they read and worked through the material in Chapter 6 in the workbook.

Learn from Experiences (*45 minutes*)

Divide the class into groups of 3-4 people each. Ask participants to turn to the Strengths Bombardment exercise page in their workbooks. (A copy of the page is also included on the Leader's CD-ROM so that you can have extra copies on hand.) The exercise chart lists fourteen 5-year periods. (Of course, not all class participants have lived through all the time periods yet!) Ask participants to list significant accomplishments or important events from at least five of the time periods on the chart. At least one of these should be a negative or disappointing experience that they came through, survived, or conquered.

Allow a total of about ten minutes for the completion of the charts.

When the charts are finished, distribute pages of blank paper or construction paper and stickers. Each participant in the group will write their name on their page. Then, in turn, each group member will read their five experiences to their group. While they listen, using their stickers, other group members will write down suggestions about strengths and traits this particular experience displays. The group will pass around the reader's page and put their stickers on the page. As they place the stickers on the page, group members verbally affirm the person with positive comments relating to the person's experiences.

For example, a person may share that they graduated from college with honors. The experience may be described as significant because the student worked his or her way through school as well as gained scholarships and paid for the entire education. It had taught the value of education and of hard work, but also had given them confidence in themselves. Other participants hearing this experience on the timeline might leave stickers saying such things as:

- Perseverance – "you stuck with it!"
- Intelligence – "you were able work a job and display academic excellence."
- Independence – "it's great that you did this on your own."

Optional Closing:

Play the selection "New Hope" on the Leader CD as the group silently meditates on how God has worked in their lives up to this moment how those experiences, good and painful, have prepared them for tomorrow.

If you are doing only a 60-minute session, end the session by praying for God to bless and heal the bad experiences of the past, and to bless and magnify the good experiences of the past. There is no assignment for next time.

If you are doing a 120-minute session, go on to Session 8 in this leader's guide now.

Experiences

We know that all things work together for good for those who love God, who are called according to his purpose.
—Romans 8:28

We all have a past. Good or bad—our experiences make us who we are today. Some people give themselves credit for the good things that happen to them, and blame God for the bad. The reality is that we aren't responsible for all the good experiences, and God doesn't cause the bad experiences to happen to us—but God does use our experiences to fulfill God's purposes. These experiences may be life experiences, ministry experiences, or simply circumstances. Let's look at an example of each of these.

Mary was devastated when her husband of twelve years said he wanted to separate. They had two young daughters, and Mary was not sure where to turn. Though a woman of faith, Mary was depressed, hurt, and angry. A friend recommended that Mary call Alison, a woman she knew in North Carolina whose husband had also asked for a separation.

When Mary finally worked up the courage to call and explained her situation, Alison immediately asked if she could pray for Mary right then, over the phone. Alison's voice seemed like that of an angel to Mary. The two women quickly became prayer partners even though a distance of one thousand miles separated them. Over the next two years as Mary's divorce finalized, Alison proved a tremendous support and encouragement for Mary. Now Mary has the opportunity to offer that same support and encouragement to other women who are trying to make it through similar circumstances. God took Mary's *life experience* (although divorce is certainly not God's wish) and used it to allow her to help other people.

Fourteen years ago, Yvonne was teaching third-grade Sunday school at a small church in Georgia (and was pretty happy doing that). When it was time to sign up for volunteer duties for the next year, a friend asked Yvonne to join the "visitation" team. The visitation team did just that—they visited all the first time visitors, welcomed them, and invited them to come to worship again.

Yvonne agreed, but became very sorry, very soon. A shy person, she found herself tongue-tied and sweaty-palmed when she walked up to a stranger's door. She was clumsy and stiff, and made others feel uncomfortable. She has said that she believes more people NEVER came back to her church after she visited than ever returned. It was a horrible experience for her. She began to think something was wrong with her, or that she was

doing something wrong. Within a few months, Yvonne began to find reasons why she couldn't go to church on her team's week to do the visitation; and then, since she felt guilt for not showing up when she was supposed to, she quit going to church at all. But God wasn't quite finished with her yet. . . .

A few years later, Yvonne and her husband, Frank, moved to Kansas City. They visited the Church of the Resurrection. They loved it and decided to join, though Yvonne was determined not to sign up for anything. She did not want another ministry experience like the last one! When she heard about Disciple Bible Study, she agreed to give it a try. Through that thirty-four weeks of study, Yvonne came to realize that we are all called to serve, but according to our spiritual gifts. It was like a lightning bolt striking her! She hadn't been doing anything wrong in her last ministry. She had been doing the wrong thing. She had not been using her spiritual gifts of Teaching and Leadership.

This experience gave Yvonne a real passion for helping others discover their spiritual gifts and to find joy in using them to serve Christ. God used a bad *ministry experience* (though God doesn't plan for God's children to have bad ministry experiences) to bring Yvonne to the place God wants her to be, serving in the way God wants her to serve, and helping other people discover God's plan for them along the way.

Several years ago, Carol's husband, Jim, was transferred to Kansas City from Chicago. Carol had lived in Chicago all her life. She held the position of Director of Community Life at her home church, which meant she was responsible for the ministries that helped connect people to the life of the church.

After the move to Kansas City, as Carol sat in the sanctuary at the Church of the Resurrection, Pastor Adam Hamilton gave a sermon on the Parable of the Talents. Carol felt the Holy Spirit urging her to talk to Adam. Since her background was in equipping ministries, especially helping people discover and use their God-given gifts and talents, maybe she could help. However, she knew that Adam was always surrounded after the service. So she prayed, "Lord, if this is your will, help me connect with Adam." Amazingly, as Carol left the sanctuary, there stood Adam, momentarily alone.

She approached him, and Adam connected Carol with Dave Robertson, then Director of Discipleship at COR. She discovered that the church had been praying for someone to help them develop a spiritual gifts ministry program. Carol began to build a team; and today, Equipping Ministries is an important part of COR. God used Carol's *life circumstances* to serve God's purposes.

When you think about it, all of our experiences—family experiences, work experiences, our relationships, our circumstances—are components of who we are and what we are prepared to do. Everything in life prepares us for our ministry, and it also allows us to be guides for others. In that sense, our experiences, good or bad, can draw us closer to God, and as we see God use them for God's purposes, we develop a better understanding of God's will for our lives.

What experiences and circumstances in your life can God use for God's purposes?

How can you use them to help others?

STRENGTHS BOMBARDMENT

Adapted from Leadership Training Network

AGE	EVENT
0-5	
6-10	
11-15	
16-20	
21-25	
26-30	
31-35	
36-40	
41-45	
46-50	
51-55	
56-60	
61-65	
66-70	

Adapted with permission from Leadership Training Network, 1- 877-LTN-LEAD
www.ltn.org. The Leadership Training Network's mission is to influence innovative church
leaders and equip people for biblical, gift-based ministry.

SESSION 8
PUTTING IT ALL TOGETHER

If you are doing four 120-minute sessions, you will pick up here immediately following the end of Session 7. You will probably wish to take a 5-minute break before starting in on the material contained here in Session 8.

If you are doing eight 60-minute sessions, Session 8 is a separate, stand-alone session.

OBJECTIVE FOR THIS SESSION:

To think about how all the S.T.R.I.D.E. components can together help us understand where God wants us to be in ministry; and, for those who feel ready, to take the next step towards one-on-one ministry placement consultations.

Prepare by reading in advance the material in the Conclusion in the workbook, and in Session 8 in the leader's guide. Read all Bible passages for yourself. Fill out the S.T.R.I.D.E. Profile form yourself. Print out and copy enough ministry position descriptions from the CD-ROM for each participant.

Watch the CD-ROM video segments, "Chapter 8, Putting It All Together" and "Conclusion." If you are using the overhead slides, either print the overheads for Session 8 for use on a projector or bring the disk for use with a computer and projector.

Make sure that you or someone else from your church is prepared to follow up with offering one-on-one ministry placement con-

sultations with those participants who wish them. It is vitally important that persons who have identified what their spiritual gifts, talents, resources, individuality, dreams, and experiences be quickly matched up with an area in which they can serve other people to the glory of God.

Materials Needed: pens or pencils; white board or newsprint with appropriate markers; Bibles; workbooks.

If You Are Starting a 60-Minute Session *(5 minutes)*

Welcome participants back and open with prayer thanking God for the opportunity to serve God through helping other people.

Review What Experiences Can Offer *(15 minutes)*

Divide participants into smaller groups of three. Instruct the small groups to allow each person five minutes in which to tell about insights they learned from the Strength Bombardment exercise at the end of Session 7.

Fill Out the Ministry Profile *(10 minutes)*

Tell participants to turn to the Ministry Profile on page 55 of the workbook. Based on all they have learned about themselves through *Serving from the Heart,* ask participants to fill out their Ministry Profile.

You may want to note on the white board or newsprint that they can locate information they wrote about themselves in previous sessions on these pages in their workbook:

Spiritual Gifts: page 15
Talents: page 32
Resources: page 34

Individuality: page 40
Dreams: page 47
Experiences: page 50

Tell them to skip over the section for "Three Possible Areas of Ministry Involvement" at this time. However, if they are, they should complete the line that begins, "I am already involved in the ministry area of . . ."

For the moment, they should hold onto their completed Ministry Profile form.

See How Matching People with Ministries Works *(25 minutes)*

Divide participants into new small groups of three to five persons. Distribute copies of the five ministry position descriptions to each participant. Each small group is now to take on the role of the Ministry Matching Team of a congregation. Their task is to talk about and come to some consensus about what kinds of spiritual gifts, talents, resources, individuality, dreams, and experiences they might look for in a person they would want to match up with each of the ministries on the sheet.

If a group has time, persons within the group may discuss to what extent they are suited to serve in one of the ministry positions described on the sheets according to the S.T.R.I.D.E. components with which they have just come up.

Close Out the Course *(5 minutes)*

Be sure that persons have marked on their Ministry Profile forms whether they want a one-on-one ministry placement consultation. Explain that if they mark "Yes," either you or someone else from the congregation will contact them to spend time going over their profile in detail and suggesting specific ways in which they might be of service within their church or community. Ask participants to pass in to you their Ministry Profile forms.

Close by asking participants who wish to do so to offer their own prayers, and conclude by praying that whatever comes of the work of the people in this course, may it be for God's glory alone.

Conclusion

For God is not unjust; he will not overlook your work and the love that you showed for his sake in serving the saints, as you still do. And we want each one of you to show the same diligence so as to realize the full assurance of hope to the very end, so that you may not become sluggish, but imitators of those who through faith and patience inherit the promises. —Hebrews 6:10-12

Most of the time, when we hear the word *minister*, we think of a professionally trained person, serving in a paid staff position in our church. Rarely do we think of members of the church as "ministers." However, this is not an accurate reflection of the way the word was used in the New Testament.

The word *minister* comes from the translation of the Greek word *diakonia* which means "act of service." The word *deacon* traces its beginning to the word *diakonos*, which means "one who serves." Sometimes the word *deacon* is used in the New Testament to refer to special servants who meet certain qualifications specified in Acts 6:1-6 and 1 Timothy 3:8-13. But the word is also used in a more universal way to refer to all Christians in other passages. For example, in Ephesians 4:12, Paul speaks of God's people being equipped for "the work of ministry." The word used here is *diakonia*. Ministry is not an office, but an act of service. *Every believer is a minister.*

> *But you are a chosen race, a royal priesthood, a holy nation, God's own people, in order that you may proclaim the mighty acts of him who called you out of darkness into his marvelous light.*
>
> —1 Peter 2:9

We believe you are called to ministry. But as you serve, stay alert to three dangers that may threaten or tempt you. One is the danger of self-reliance and/or self-sufficiency. We sometimes get confused about the "ownership" of our gifts, talents, resources, and so forth, thinking that they "belong" to us to use as we wish, rather than treating them as gifts given by God. This can lead us to use what God has given us for our own benefit, or might cause us to rely solely upon ourselves in ministry. The attitude we need to cultivate with regard to our gifts is one of stewardship, not ownership; and rather than keeping those gifts to ourselves, or relying only on our own abilities and power, we need to place ourselves in a position of dependence on God.

The second danger is that of burning out in your ministry. Burnout usually comes from one of three sources. One comes when we don't have enough instruction or guidance to feel confident that we are doing what we are sup-

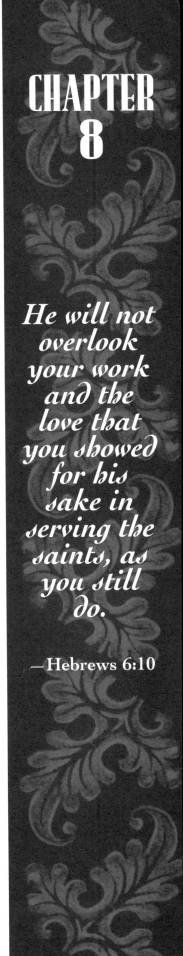

He will not overlook your work and the love that you showed for his sake in serving the saints, as you still do.

—Hebrews 6:10

posed to be doing. Persons with a higher need for stability in their individuality are especially susceptible to this kind of burnout. If this kind of burnout seems to be happening to you, ask for more guidance, or shift to a different form of service quickly.

A second source of burnout comes when we don't support our own ministry with time with God. We need to tend to our relationship with God even more carefully than a person might tend a garden. Regular worship, daily prayer, Bible study and Christian fellowship all nourish a person's spirit so that one can survive the times of dryness and conflict that inevitably will arise during Christian ministry.

A third source of burnout comes with boredom. Sometimes we have been at a task too long. We need to be refreshed, have a change of pace, learn or try something new. And it is okay to ask to be relieved from a ministry that you have been doing so that you can take on a completely different project or task, or simply take a sabbatical—a sabbath (which, after all, is a good biblical term)—from the work you have been doing.

In other words, if you feel burnout coming on, ask for the help you need. Don't try to tough it out alone. God has placed you within the Church among other Christians for a reason—so that you might support one another and bear one another's burdens!

Now, to the third danger: Please don't fall prey to the temptation of pride and become a so-called super-Christian. Because you have a certain gift or have more of a gift than someone else or can do something better than someone else, don't ever think that you are better than they. God loves all of us the same. Your gifts are tools for you to use for God's glory, to lift up all God's people, and to build up God's Kingdom.

Beyond these dangers, though, the service of God is a beautiful, wonderful life. It is the essence of true worship. For it is as we live to serve God in the helping of God's people and the building of God's Kingdom that we truly give God the glory that is due. Nothing pleases God better than for us to use what has been given to us to do exactly that.

Find out what it is that God designed you to do—and then do it! We are all uniquely created, individually gifted children of God. God has a plan and purpose for your life. Trying to be something you are not is a no-win strategy. God has given you gifts according to God's will, and placed you in the body as God has determined. When you discover your S.T.R.I.D.E. and put it into action, you will find joy. You'll be fulfilling God's plan for your life!

As we climb the Spiritual Summits (growing in our faith—higher up and farther in), the journey is so much more fulfilling if we are in-step with our own, unique, God-given S.T.R.I.D.E.

May God bless you as you seek to know God better and follow God.

And Jesus came and said to them, "All authority in heaven and on earth has been given to me. Go therefore and make disciples of all nations, baptizing them in the name of the Father and of the Son and of the Holy Spirit, and teaching them to obey everything that I have commanded you. And remember, I am with you always, to the end of the age."

—Matthew 28:18-20

Ministry Profile

Request Consultation_____

NAME _____ *Day Phone:* _____

E-mail: _____ *Evening Phone* _____

INSTRUCTOR: _____ *Class Ending Date:* _____

SPIRITUAL GIFTS - my three highest scoring Spiritual Gifts (in order) are:

_____

_____

_____

TALENTS - _____
_____

RESOURCES - _____
_____

INDIVIDUALITY - I believe my style is:
_____

DREAMS - I sense I have a Passion for: _____

EXPERIENCES - _____
_____

THREE POSSIBLE AREAS OF MINISTRY INVOLVEMENT

_____

_____

_____

I AM ALREADY INVOLVED IN THE MINISTRY AREA OF -

_____

Group Roster

Name:

_____

Address:

_____

_____

Telephone:

_____

Email:

_____

Requests consultation
(for service placement) _____

Name:

_____

Address:

_____

_____

Telephone:

_____

Email:

_____

Requests consultation
(for service placement) _____

Name:

_____

Address:

_____

_____

Telephone:

_____

Email:

_____

Requests consultation
(for service placement) _____

Name:

_____

Address:

_____

_____

Telephone:

_____

Email:

_____

Requests consultation
(for service placement) _____

Name:

_____

Address:

_____

_____

Telephone:

_____

Email:

_____

Requests consultation
(for service placement) _____

Name:

_____

Address:

_____

_____

Telephone:

_____

Email:

_____

Requests consultation
(for service placement)

Name:

_____

Address:

_____

_____

Telephone:

_____

Email:

_____

Requests consultation
(for service placement) _____

Name:

_____

Address:

_____

_____

Telephone:

_____

Email:

_____

Requests consultation
(for service placement) _____

Name:

_____

Address:

_____

_____

Telephone:

_____

Email:

_____
Requests consultation
(for service placement) _____

Name:

_____

Address:

_____

_____

Telephone:

_____

Email:

_____
Requests consultation
(for service placement) _____

Name:

_____

Address:

_____

_____

Telephone:

_____

Email:

_____
Requests consultation
(for service placement) _____

Name:

_____

Address:

_____

_____

Telephone:

_____

Email:

_____
Requests consultation
(for service placement) _____